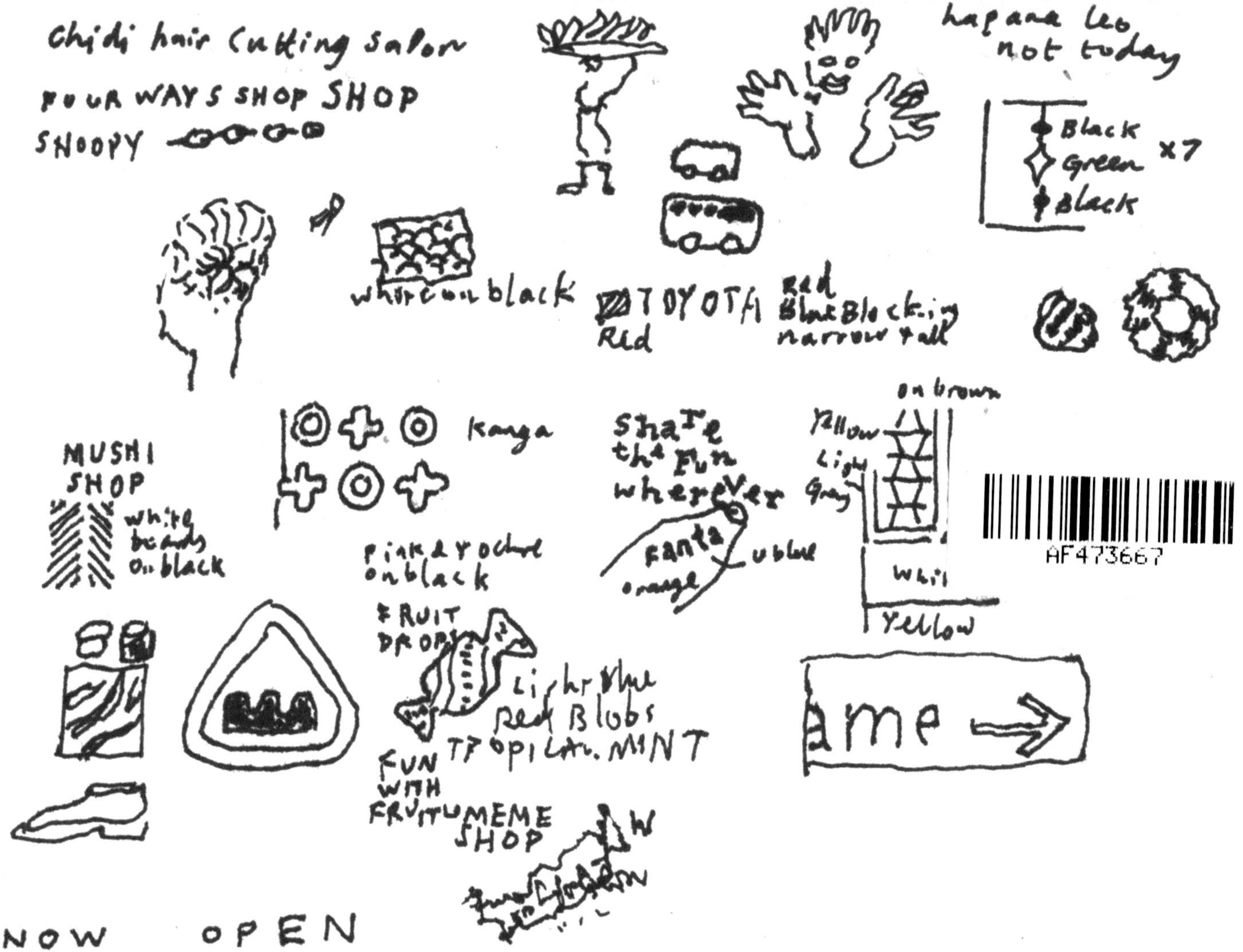

Chidi hair Cutting salon

FOUR WAYS SHOP SHOP

SNOOPY

hapana leo
not today

Black
Green
Black
x7

white on black

TOYOTA
Red

Red
Blue Blocking
narrow tall

on brown
Yellow
Light Gray
White
Yellow

MUSHI
SHOP
white
beads
on black

Kanga

Share
the Fun
wherever

Fanta
orange
blue

pink & ochre
on black

FRUIT
DROPS

Light blue
red Blobs
TROPICAL MINT

FUN
WITH
FRUITUMEME
SHOP

ame →

NOW OPEN

Humphrey Ocean

AFRICA

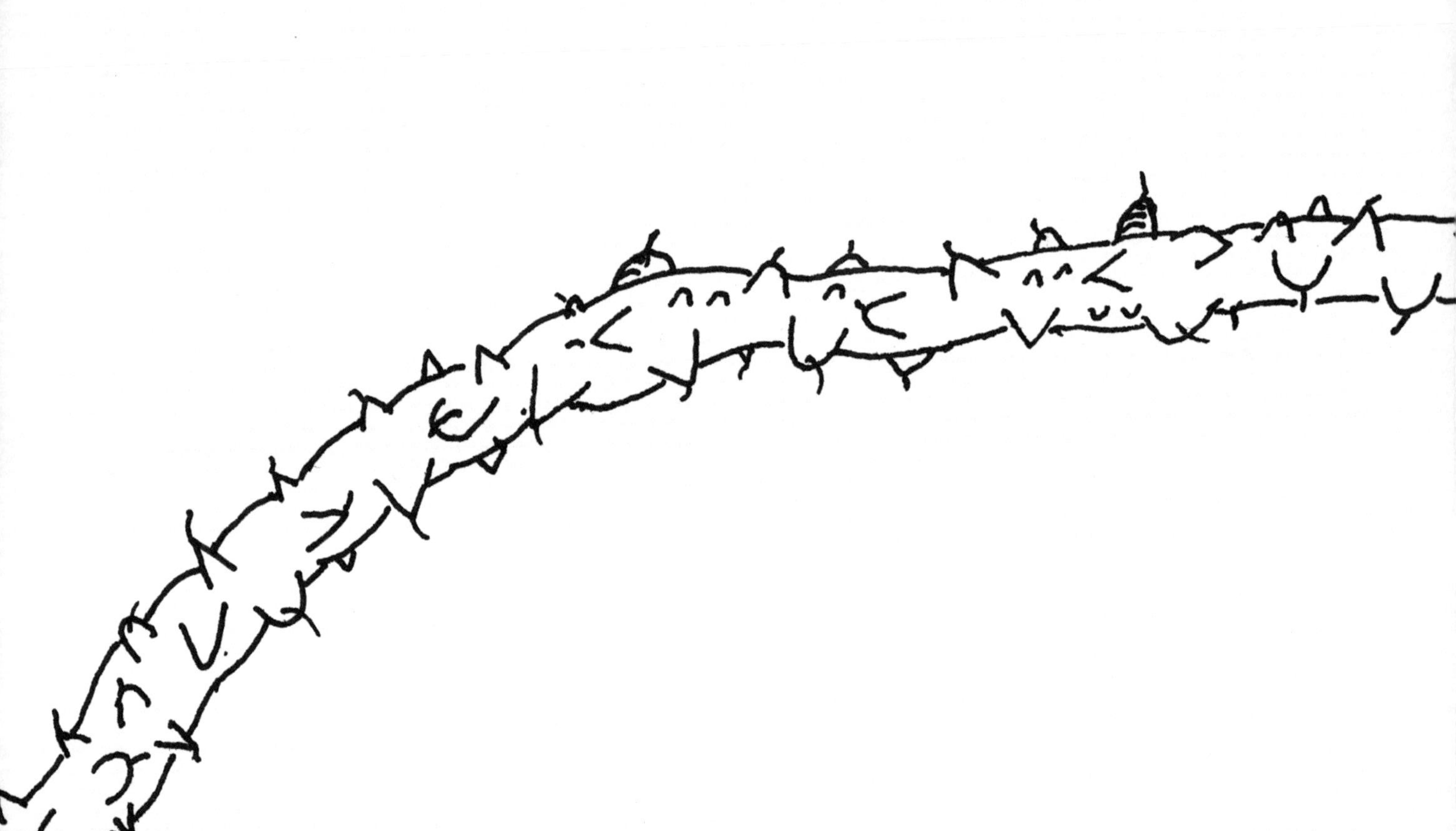

Royal Academy of Arts

Humphrey Ocean

AFRICA

This is not a book about Africa; it is my Africa. Even to say that is an impertinence. It is a place so vast and various that, as Ryszard Kapuściński says, 'Except as a geographical appellation, Africa does not exist.' And I only went to a tiny bit of it. Kenya first, and it changed my life. Then twice to next-door Tanzania, as different as could be and no less affecting. After that, five more times to Kenya, over towards Karen by the Ngong Hills.

On my first flight there, Brussels to Nairobi, the journey was almost complete when we stopped at Entebbe, like a bus picking up passengers. The doors opened, warm tropical night air flooded in, followed by Ugandans, some quiet and sombre, others laughing, and soon everyone was greeted. In a twinkling, our international air-conditioned colossus was now local transport. I had arrived before I was there.

I was going to see my sister Rachel, who had lived in Africa a long time. After a spell in Tchirozerine in Niger in the 1970s she went to live in East Africa. By 1997 she was in a small village several miles north of Nairobi, with a church and a school, on the edge of the Rift Valley. Ten days was all I could manage. Everyone, apart from Rachel, was aghast: 'Ten days?' I wouldn't see anything. 'Stay for three months, or longer!' But in the end, back at home, the sketchbook I had drawn and written in opened out and stretched the rather short time.

It was never my intention to make paintings here in England from what I had done there. How could I? The drawings are local, made on the spot, a riposte. I have enough on my plate reading the runes in my more familiar West Norwood, Sydenham and Forest

Hill: the haircuts, shrines, net curtains and alloy wheels. Something, though, did come back with me, as well as eight sketchbooks. More and more I notice people anywhere and everywhere do the same things, just in a different accent. Banana beer at a roadside kiosk covered in painted signs. A bump down a track to Elmenteita to see flamingos hover in the dazzling salt lake just under the Equator. True, you don't see that every day. Or, more simply, how the lush kitchen garden halfway up Kilimanjaro, where I stayed the second and third time, is cultivated. Ah! so they do it like *that*.

As I was sitting in the grass one afternoon, minding my own business and overlooking the Rift Valley, a schoolboy of about eight or nine, still in uniform, came over, curious. He sat on the ground next to me and talked. After a while he pulled from his pocket a twist of tinfoil, opened it and offered to share his evening meal: ugali, a few beans and a mango. The gesture alone was enough but ugali, a white maize meal that goes with anything and everything or just on its own, had become my favourite African staple. Even better, the compressed wedge he began breaking up was still warm and smoky from the charcoal-boiled water it had been cooked in. We ate gazing out over the wide and ancient turf, almost certainly where human existence began, him taking it all for granted. He then continued to watch and hum, and hummed a bit more. And that was it, he had had enough. Getting up to go, he said, 'Why isn't it?' Or at least I think he did.

There is no answer to that. The following pages are me wondering.

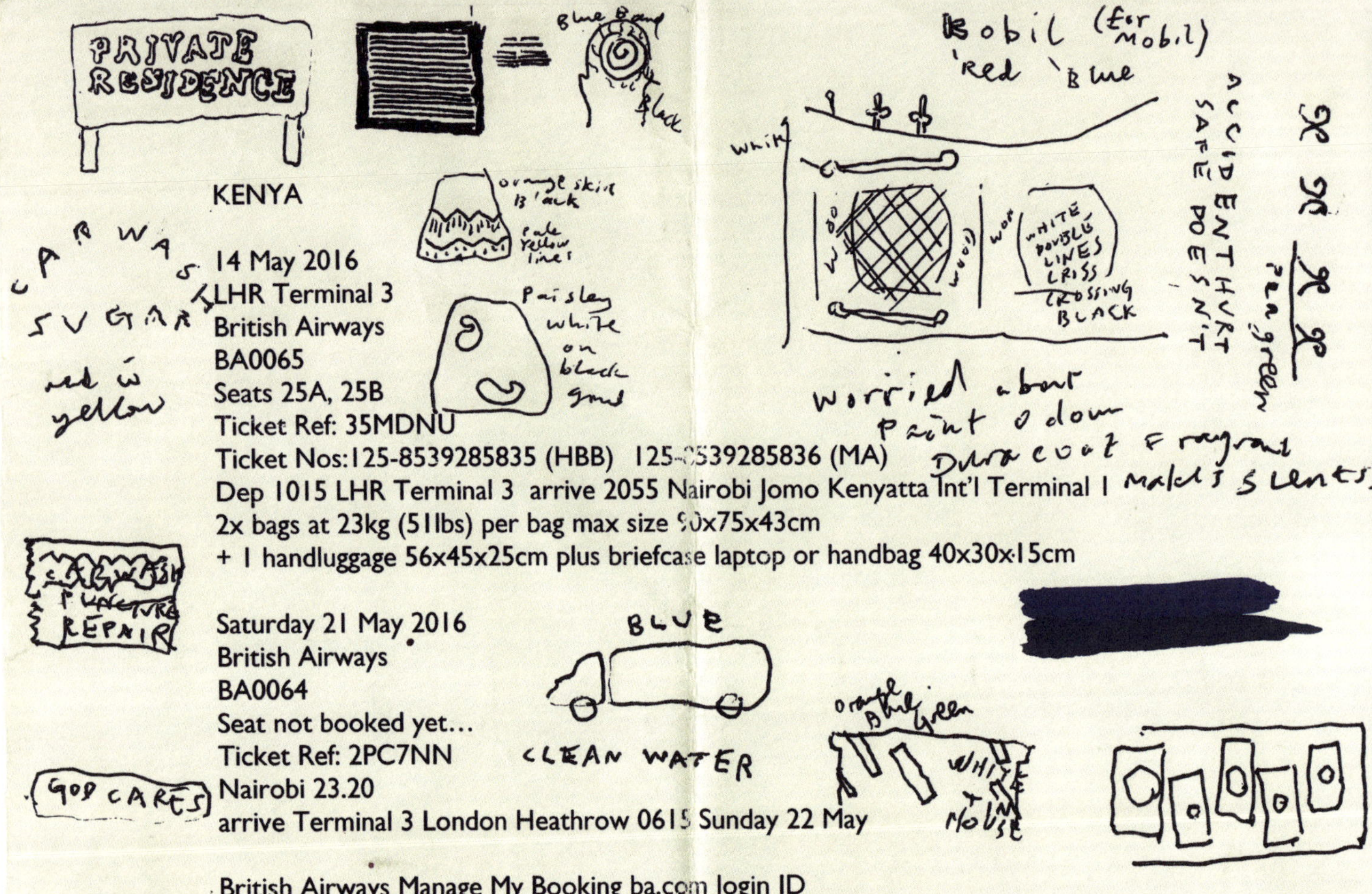

KENYA

14 May 2016
LHR Terminal 3
British Airways
BA0065
Seats 25A, 25B
Ticket Ref: 35MDNU
Ticket Nos:125-8539285835 (HBB) 125-8539285836 (MA)
Dep 1015 LHR Terminal 3 arrive 2055 Nairobi Jomo Kenyatta Int'l Terminal 1
2x bags at 23kg (51lbs) per bag max size 90x75x43cm
+ 1 handluggage 56x45x25cm plus briefcase laptop or handbag 40x30x15cm

Saturday 21 May 2016
British Airways
BA0064
Seat not booked yet…
Ticket Ref: 2PC7NN
Nairobi 23.20
arrive Terminal 3 London Heathrow 0615 Sunday 22 May

British Airways Manage My Booking ba.com login ID

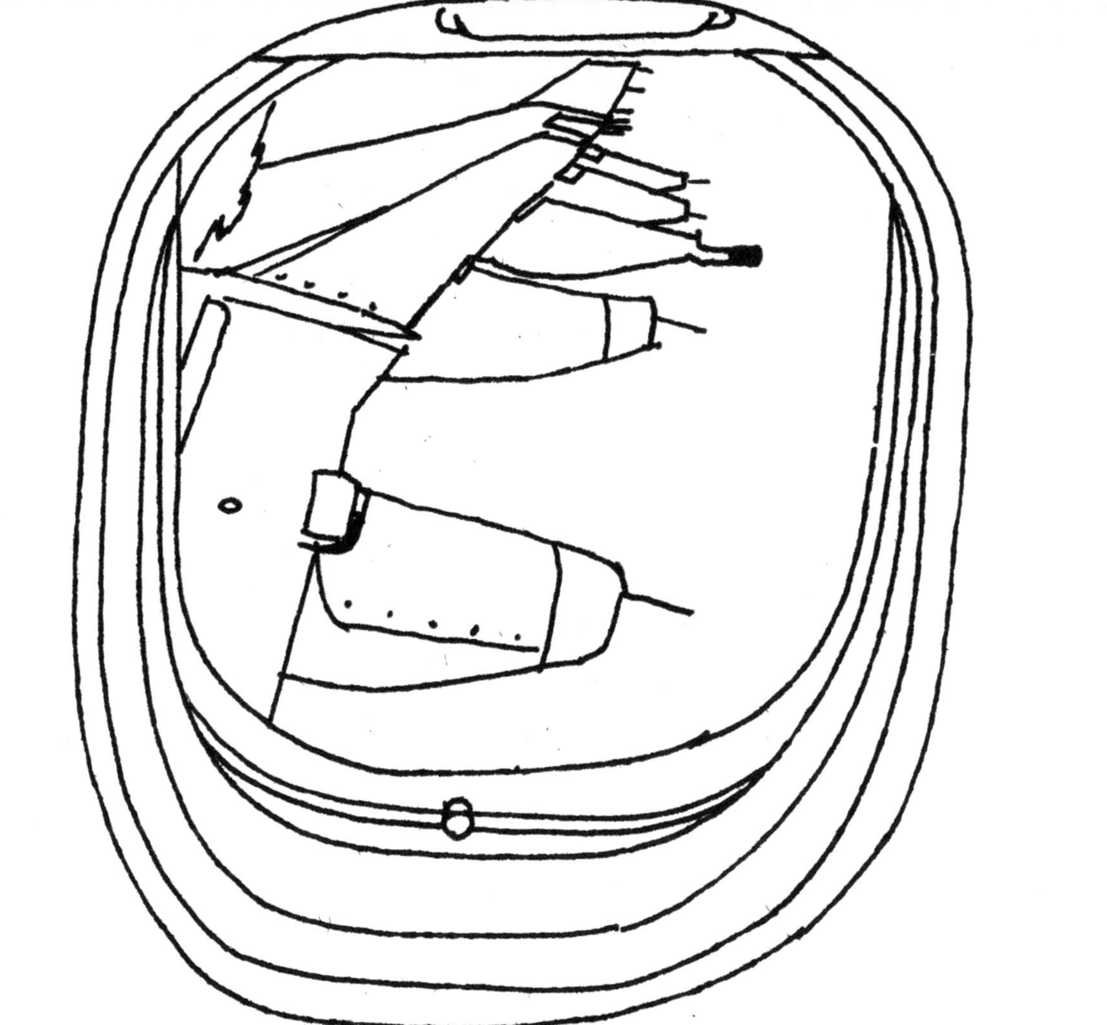

REPUBLIC OF KENYA ENTRY DECLARATION FORM

AIR	✓	SEA		RAIL		ROAD		LAKE	

OCCUPATION

FLIGHT NO

SURNAME

NATIONALITY

OTHER NAMES

REASON FOR ENTRY SIGNATURE

PLACE AND DATE OF ISSUE

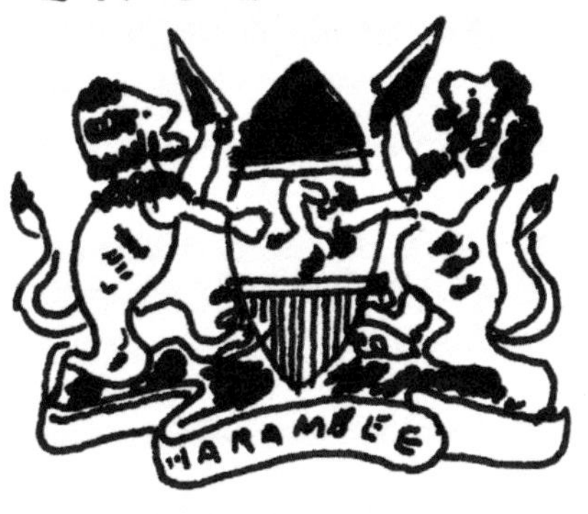

FULL ADDRESS IN KEN

COUNTRY OF RESIDENC

CATEGORY R NO

CODE IMMIGRATION

SECURITY OFFICER

FOR OFFICIAL USE ONLY T445

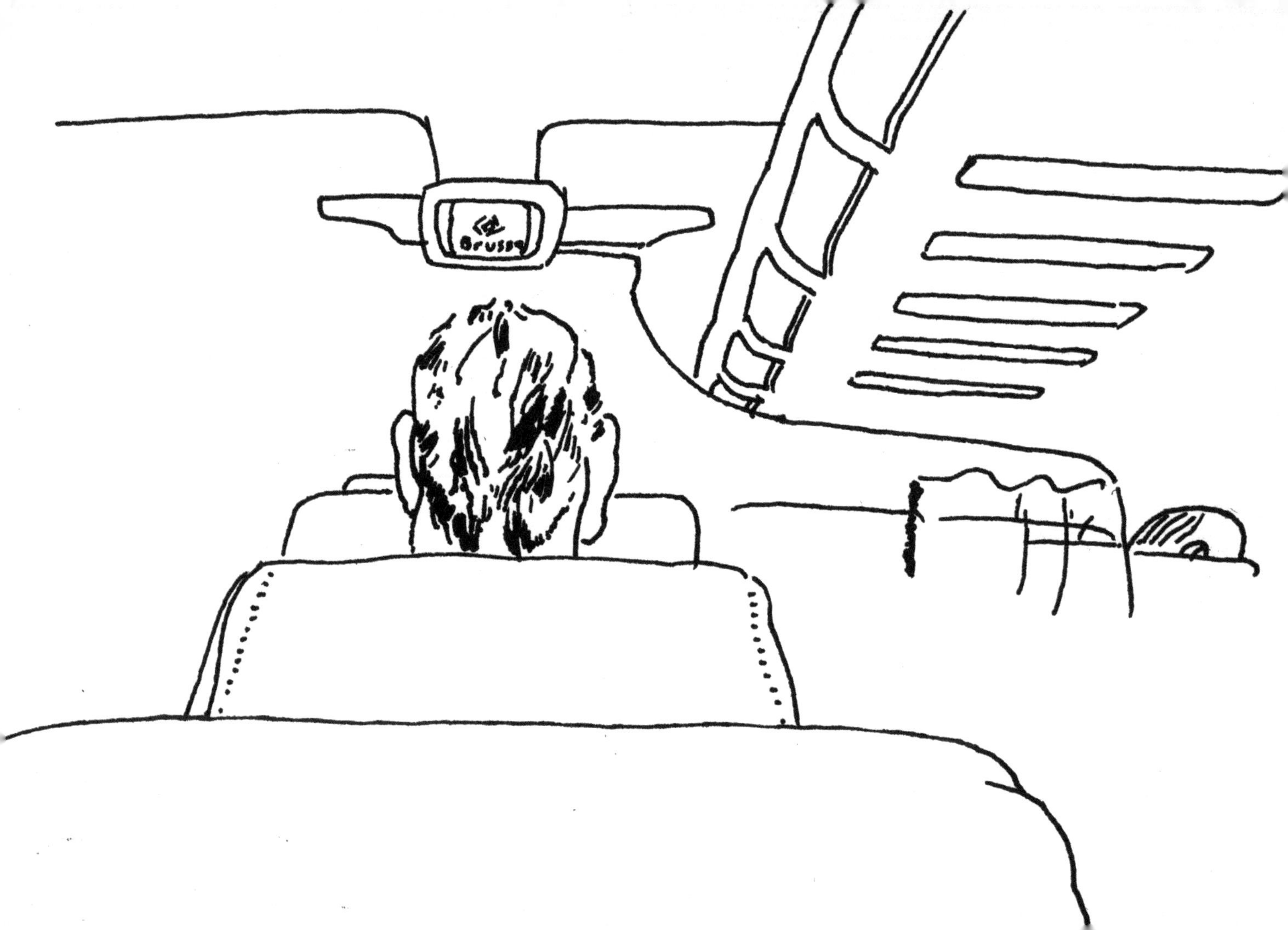
Brusse

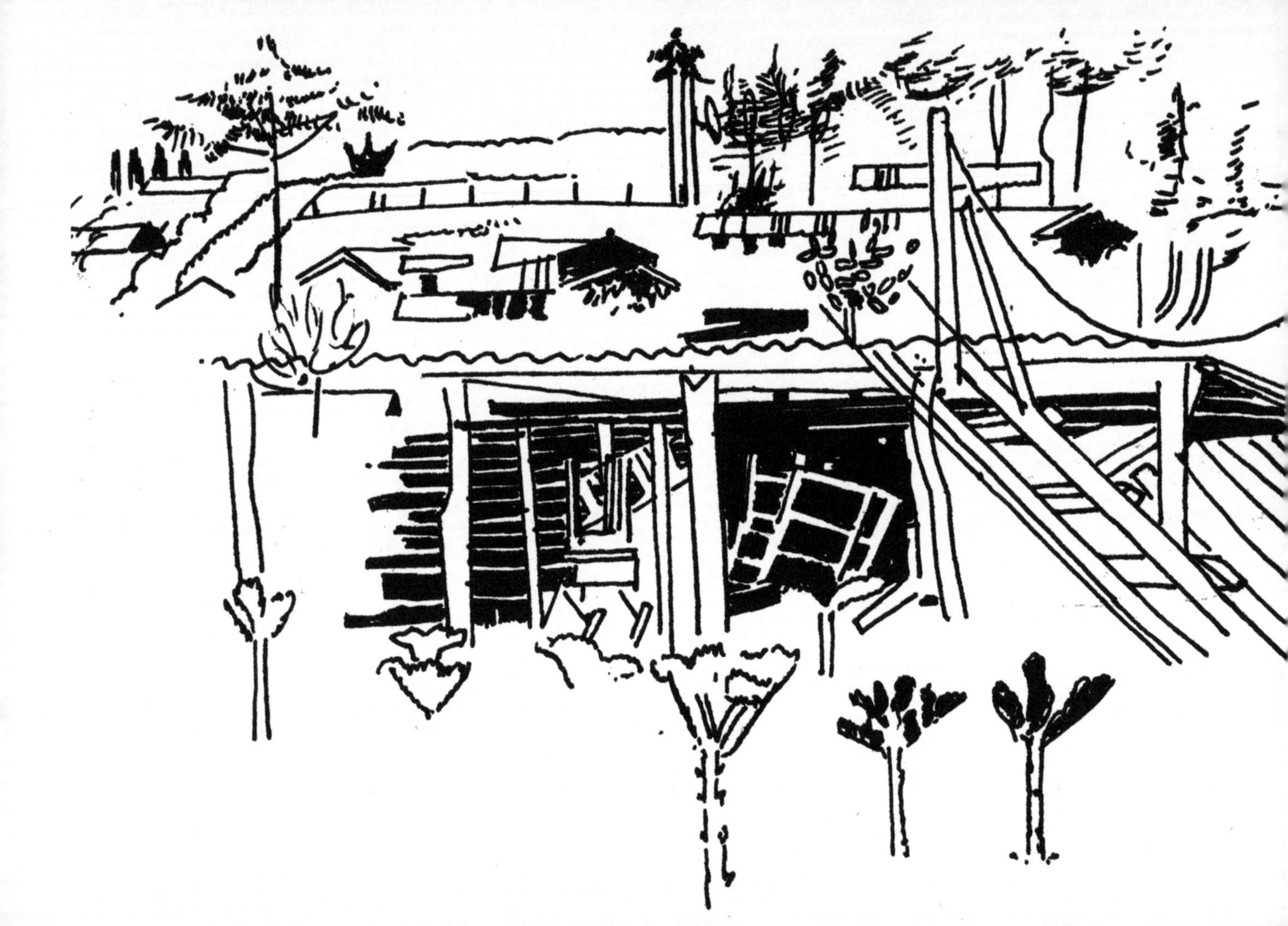

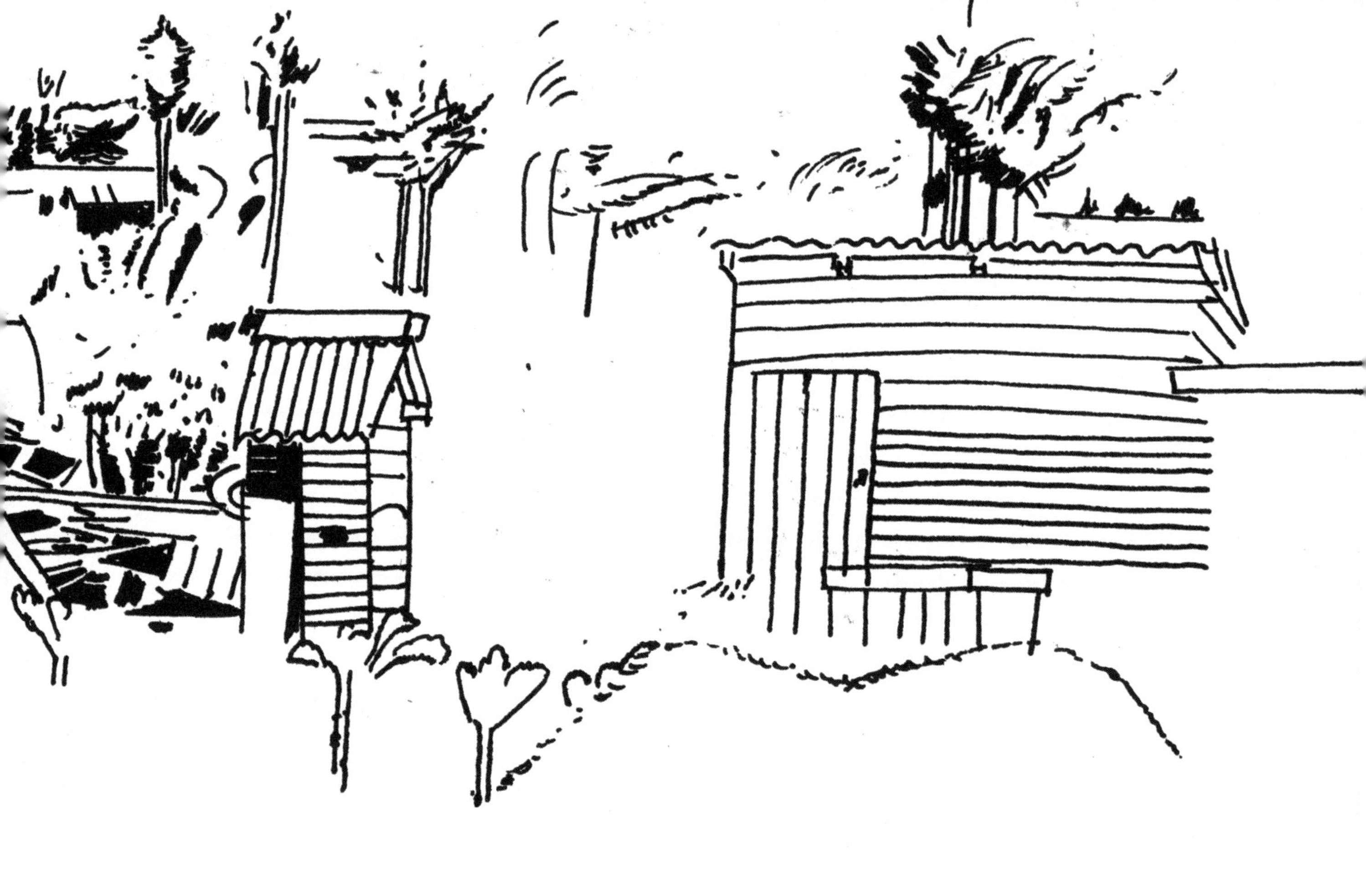

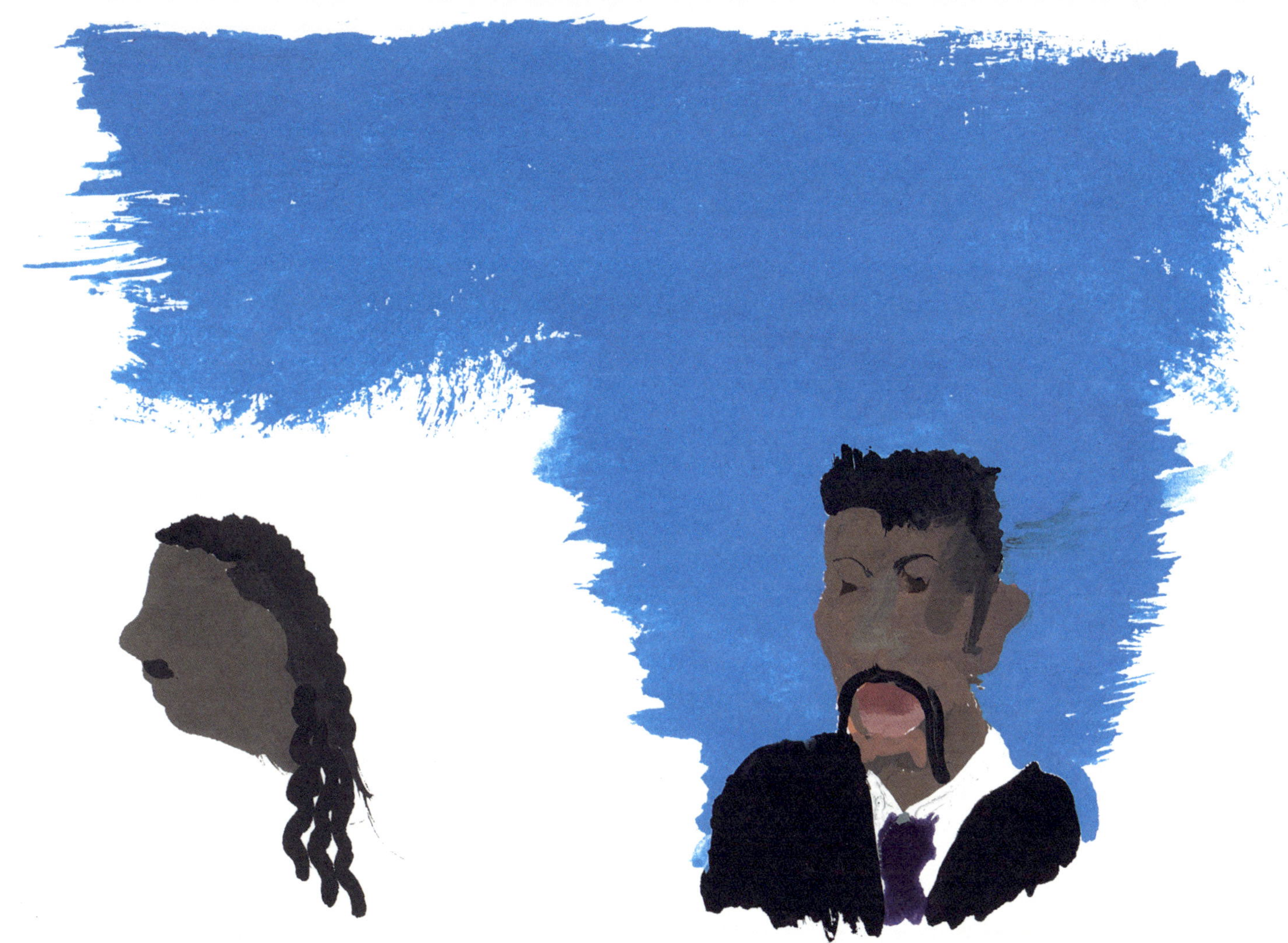

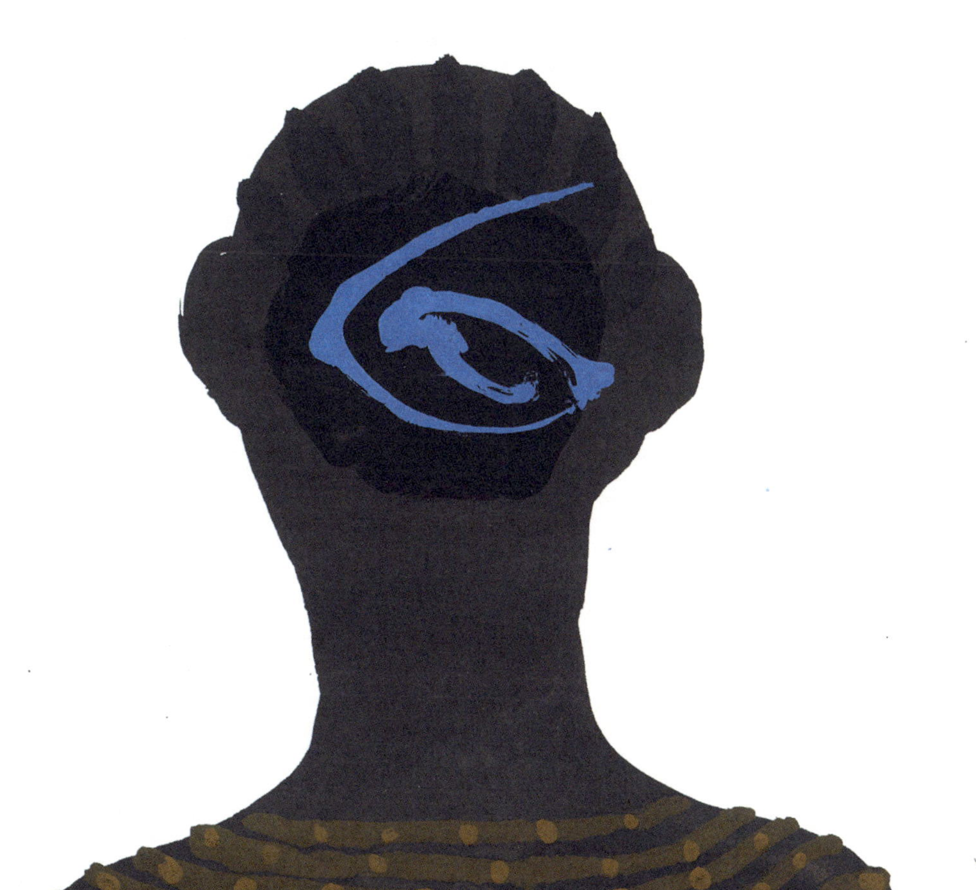

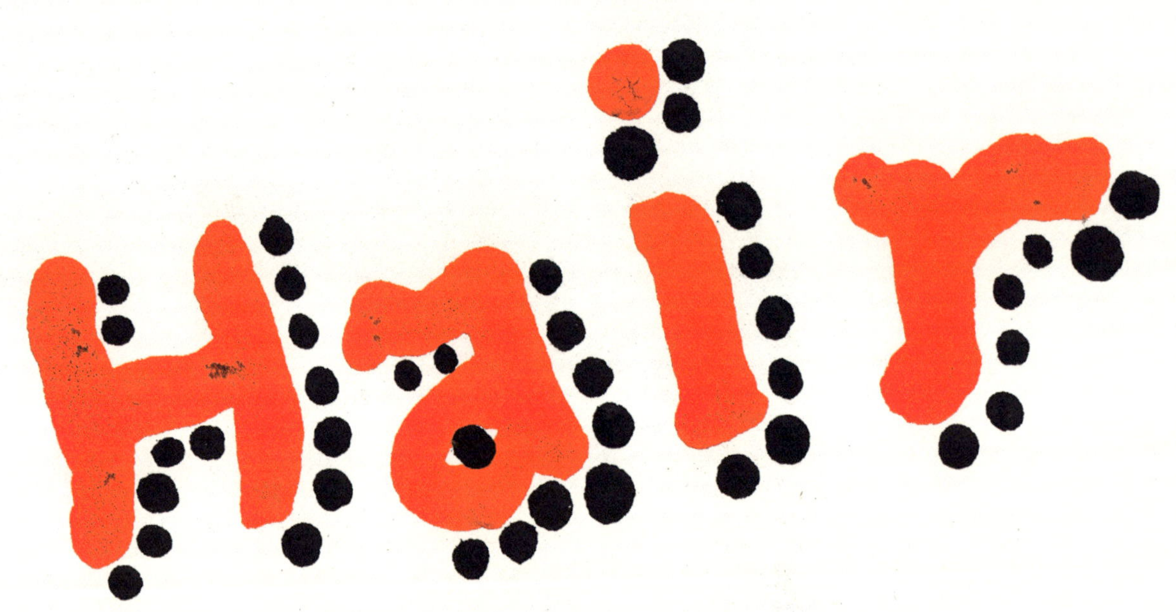
Hair

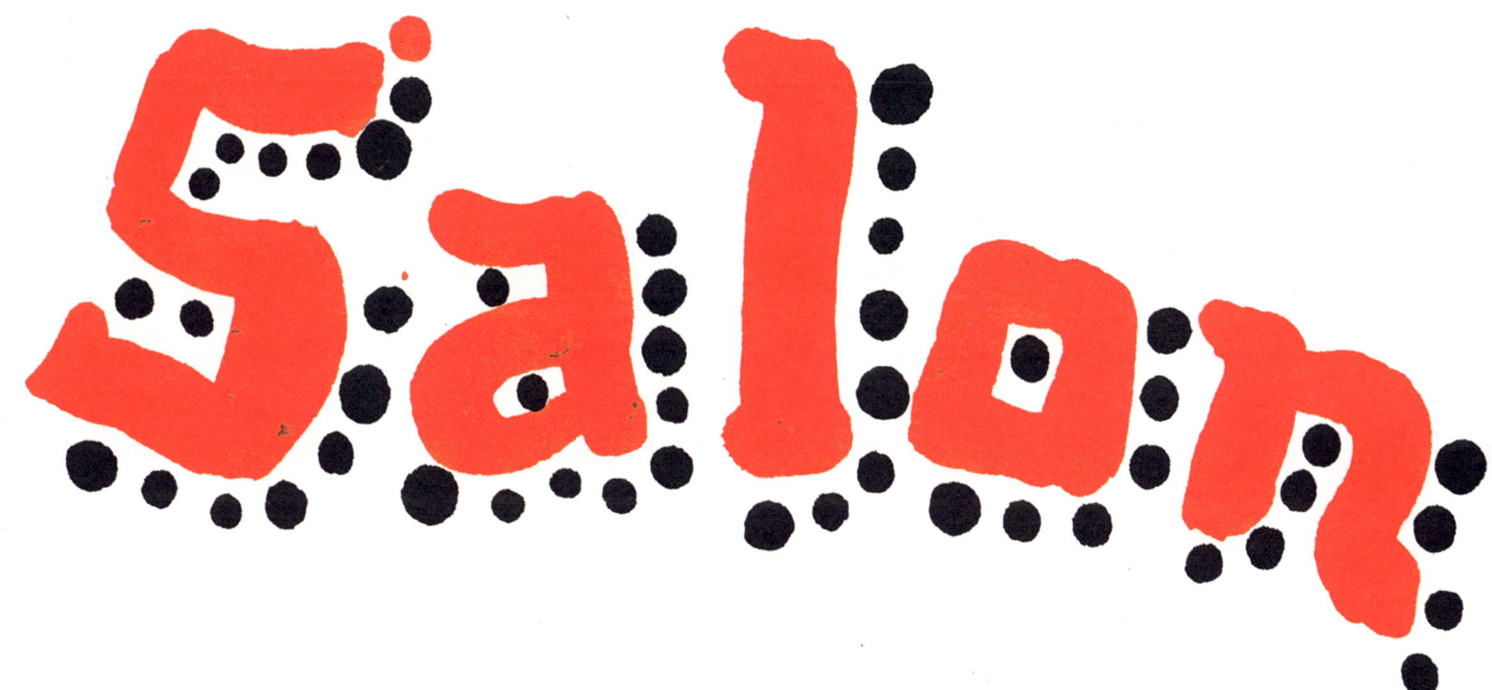
Salon

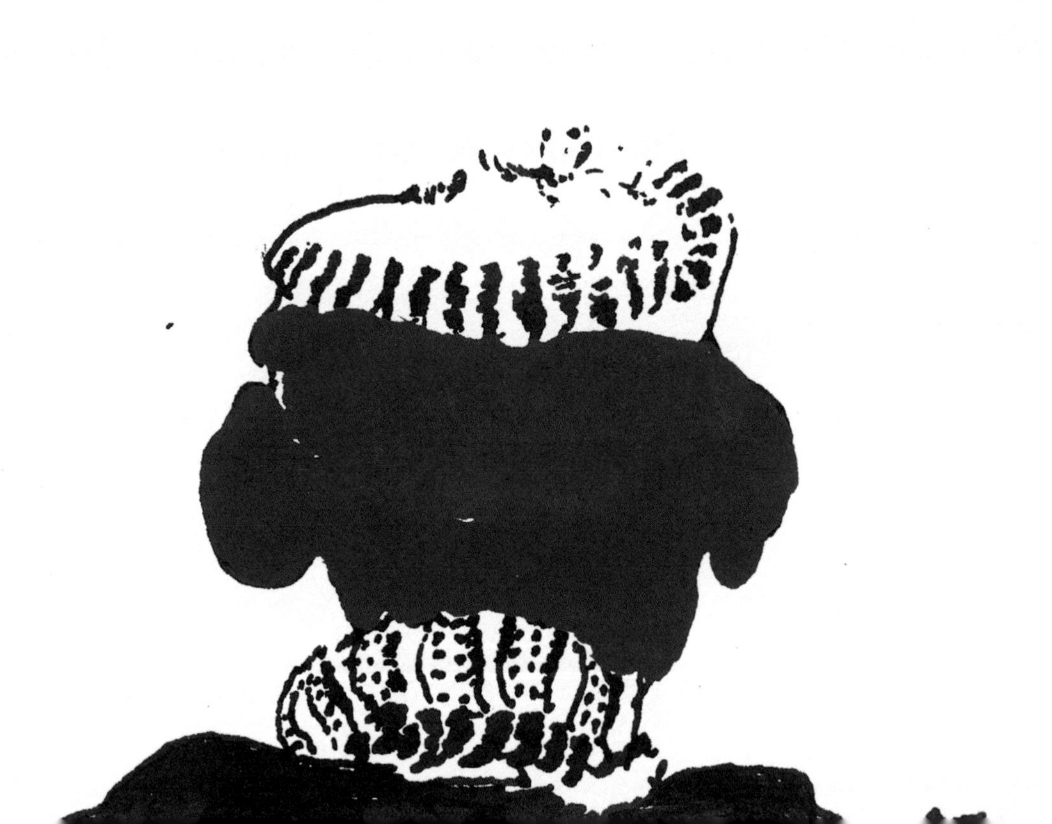

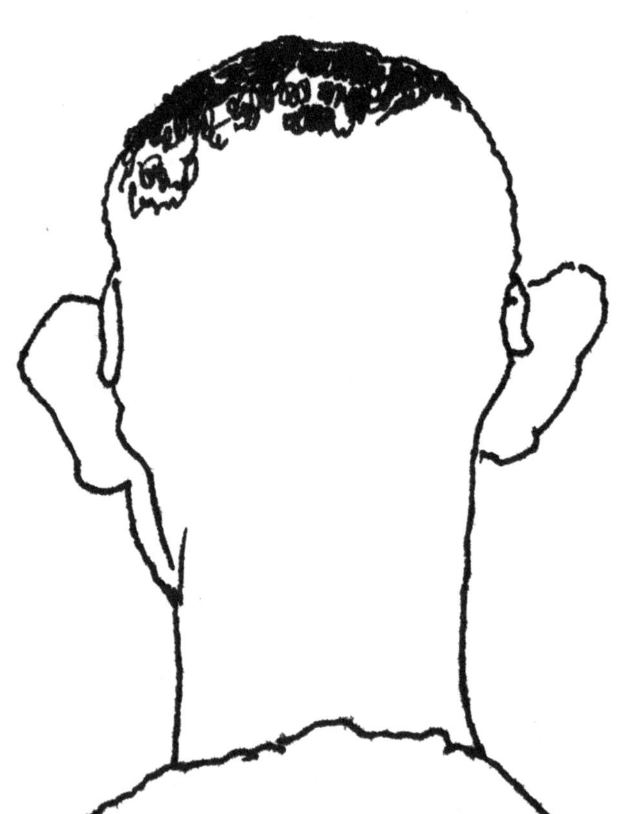

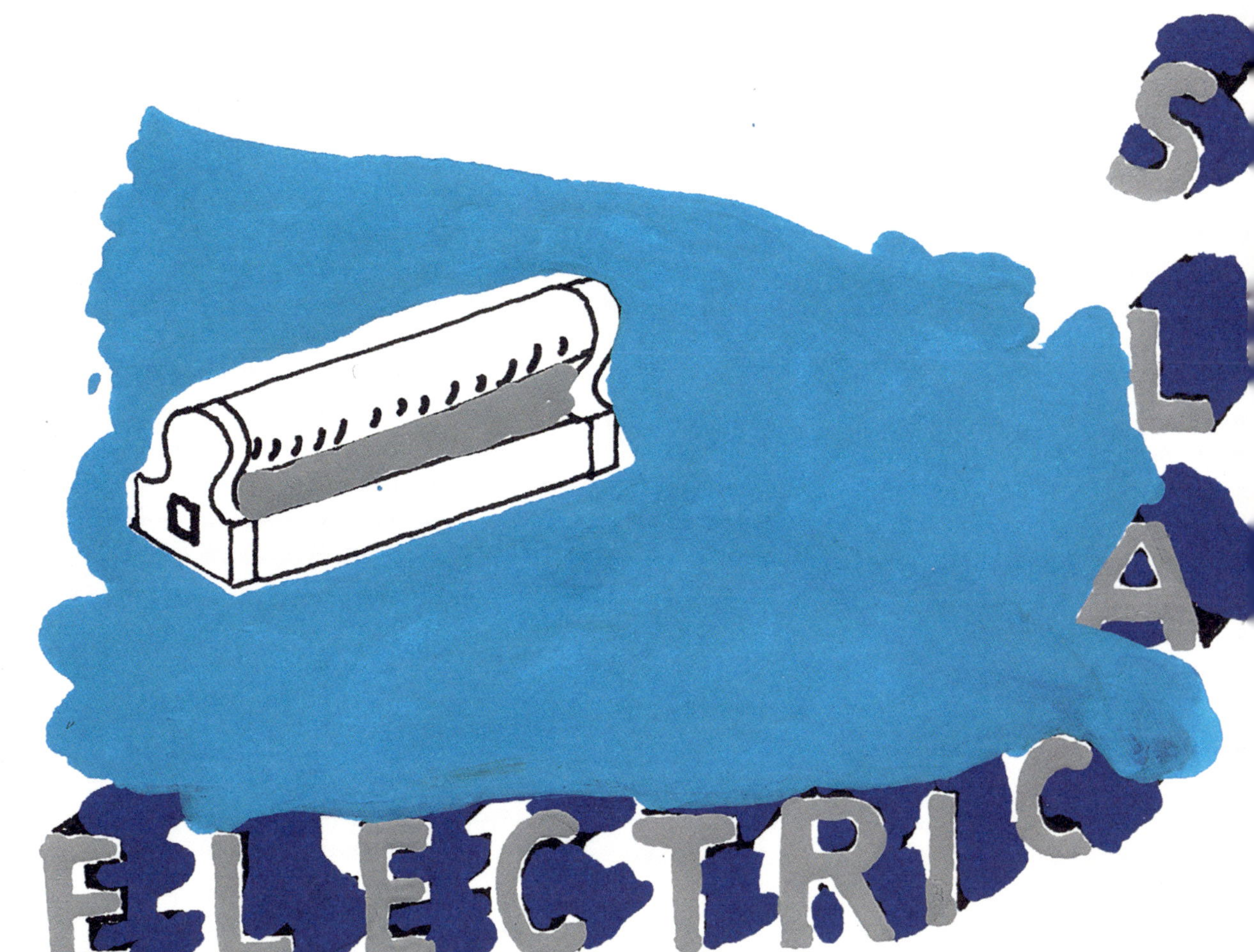
S
L
A
ELECTRIC

SPARKLING WASH!

GITHERI

BEANS

MAIZE

CARROTS

POTATOES

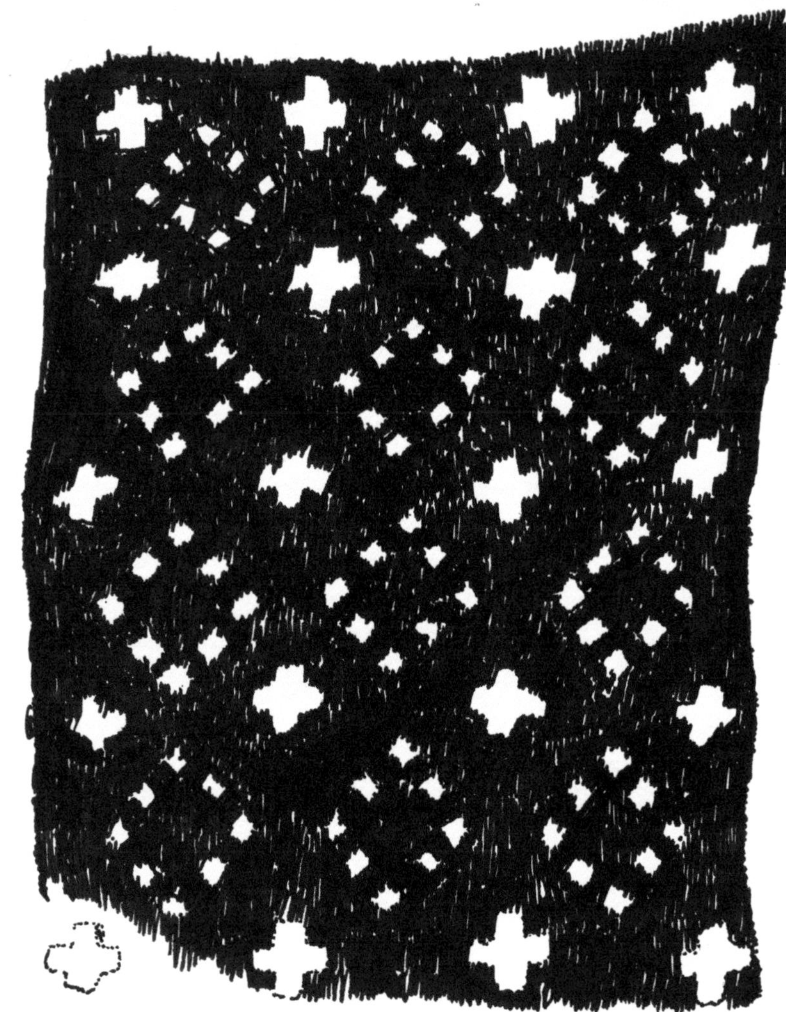

POST OFFICE

After picking up Rachel's passport wch we near forgot and handi
in our passes - the trial finished for the day at one o'clock
resume again nine thirty monday morning. officials in Tanzan
avoid working Friday afternoon unless entirely necessary. we
went to the cultural Heritage Centre where for the price of
a soda (600 Tsh each) we sat at the bar and ate our picnic
cheese rolls boiled eggs bananas. Then went round CHC wch is really
a tourist trap disguised as a free museum. It is run by an Indi
(photos of Bill clinton's visit displayed) and has some good Makonde
sculpture, a lot not so good, models of animals a Masai house (which
is used by the nightwatchman, ashes of a fire on the floor) but
the central circular building is stuffed with objects in the courtyar
and the main building is a shop. Mainly stuff specially made lots of
it of no special interest but I bought an old black and white blanket
which was unusual, and I daresay unusually overpriced. They wer
doing plenty of trade, it is obviously on the serengety Ngorongoro circuit

MANCHESTER H

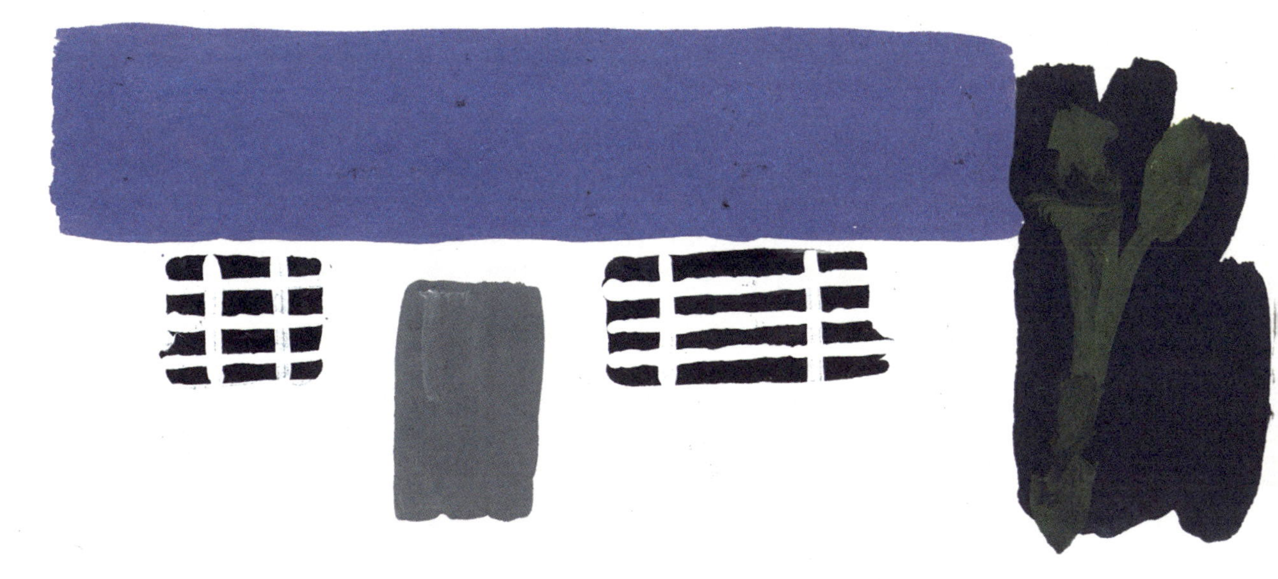

AIRCUTZ

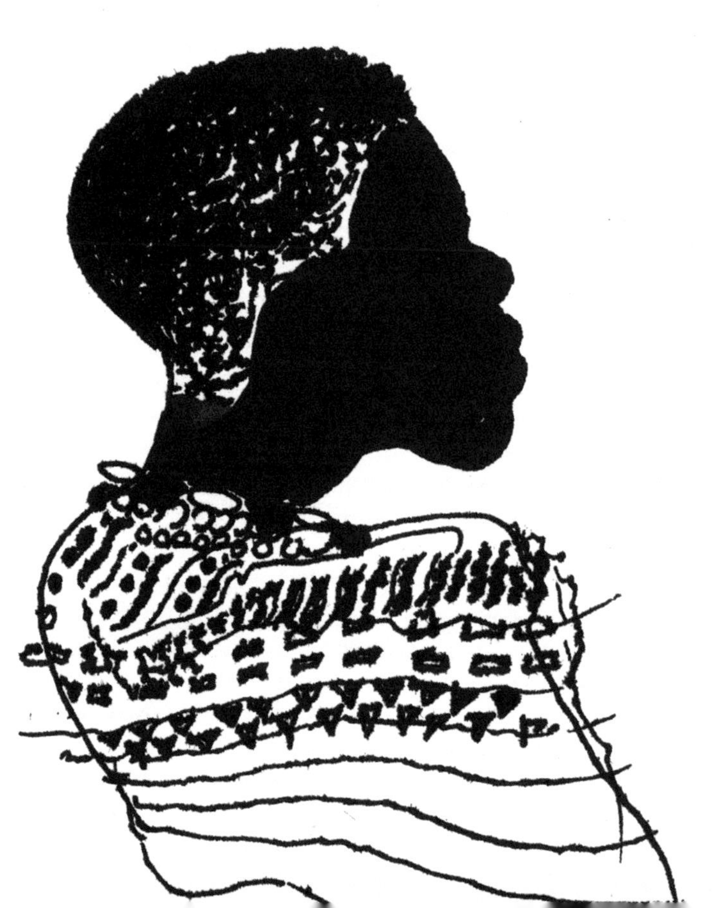

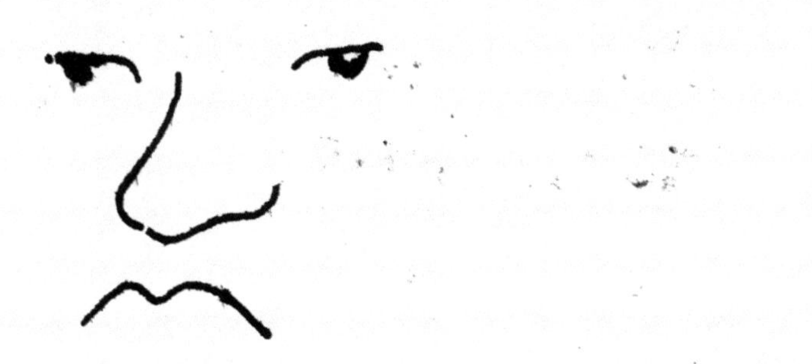

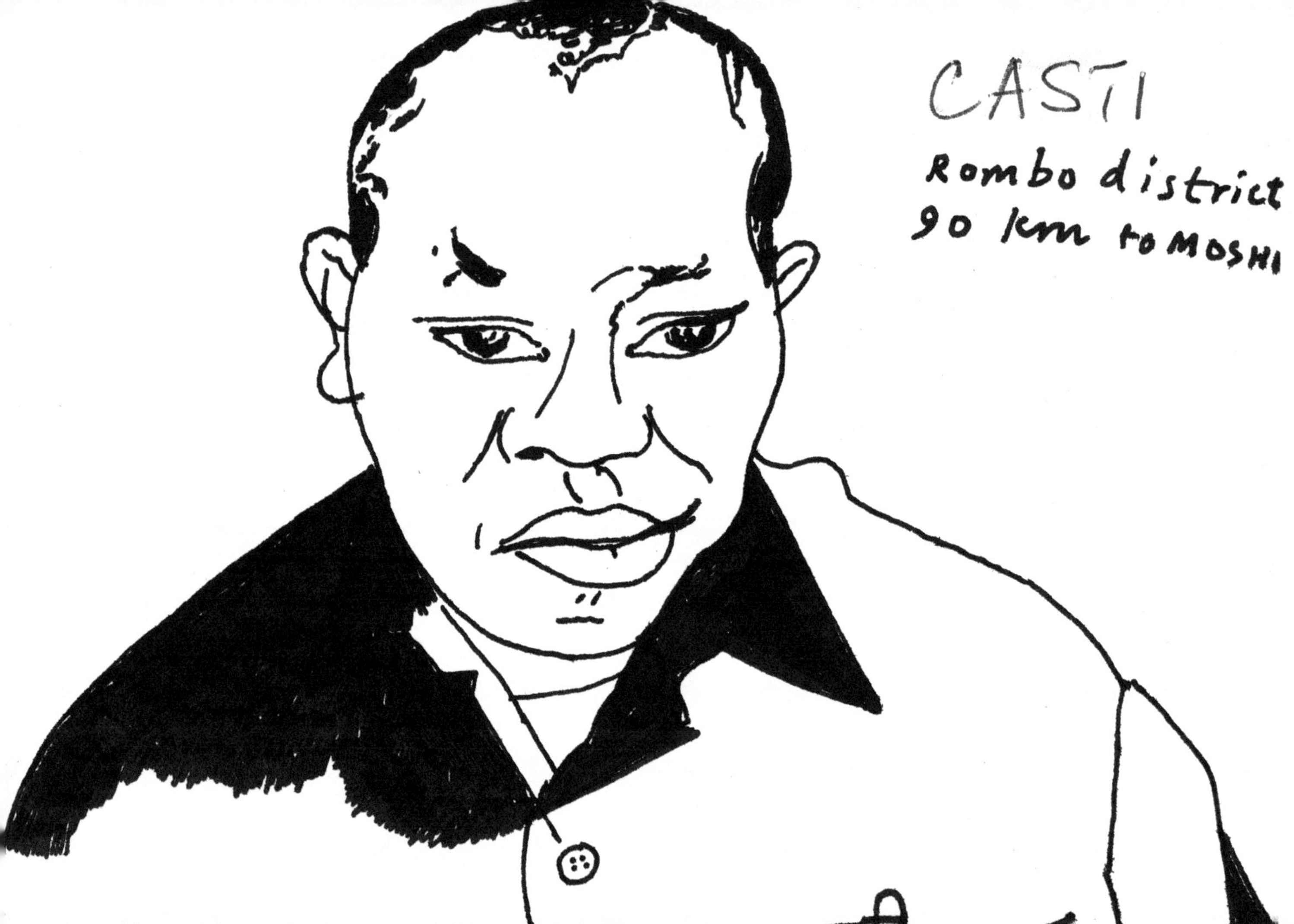
CASTI
Rombo district
90 km to MOSHI

TOY

OTA%

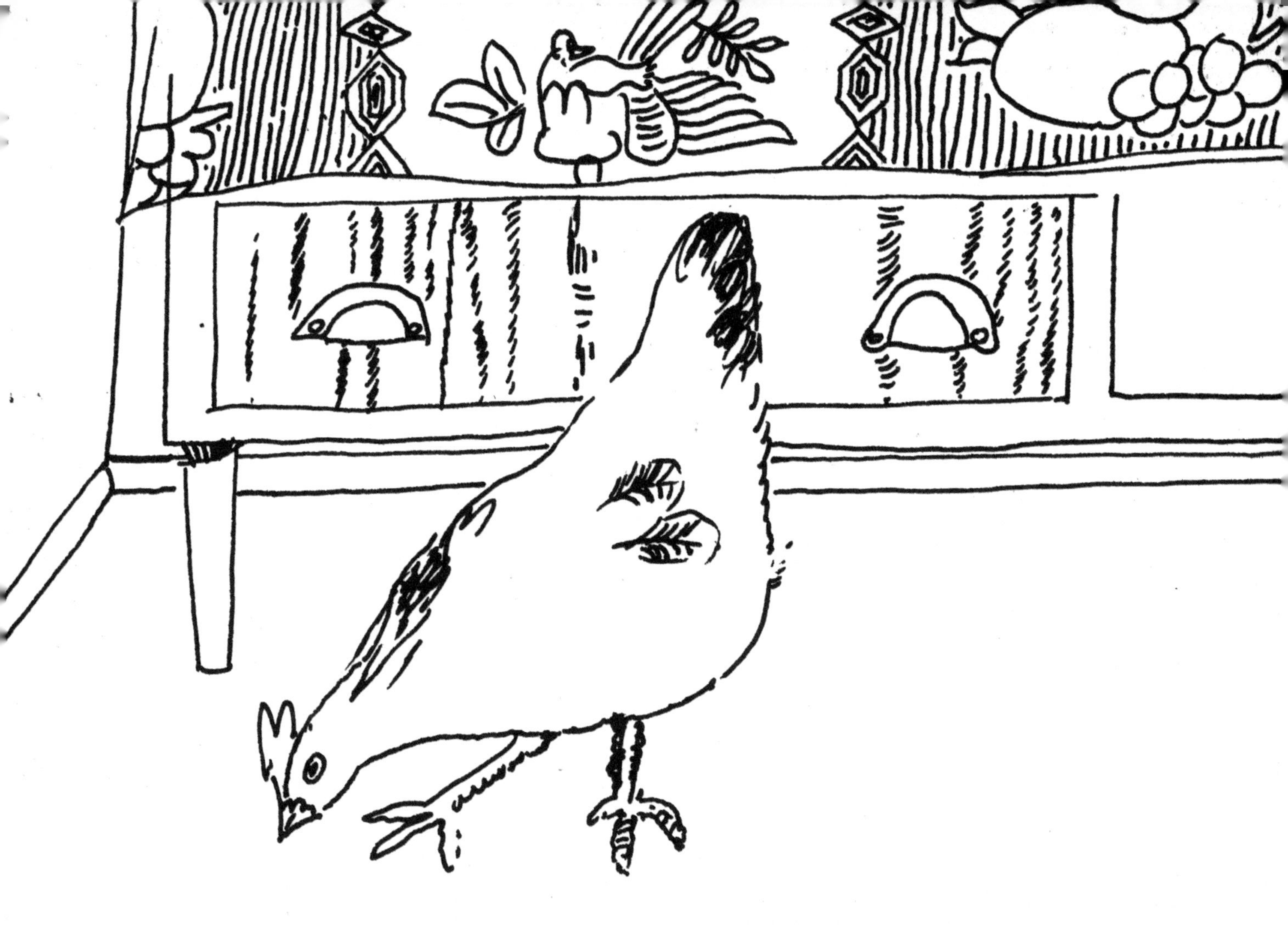

Shiro
HAIR

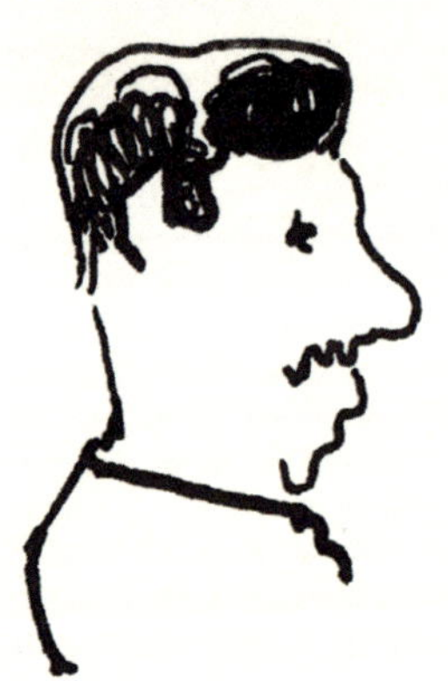

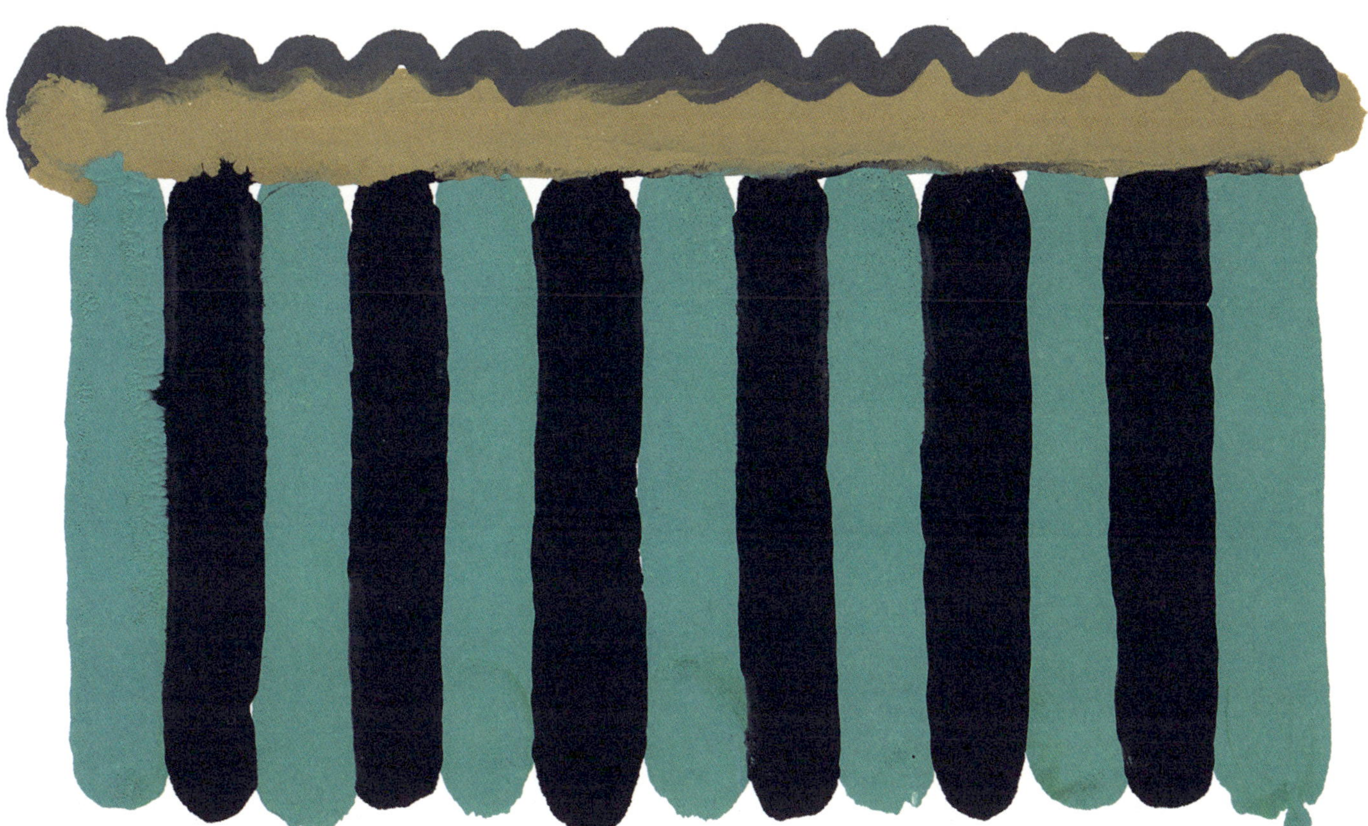

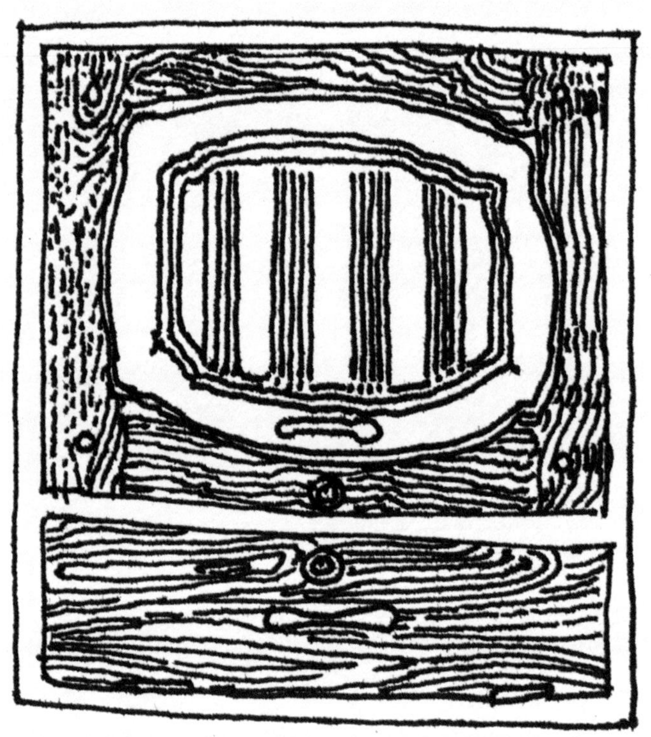

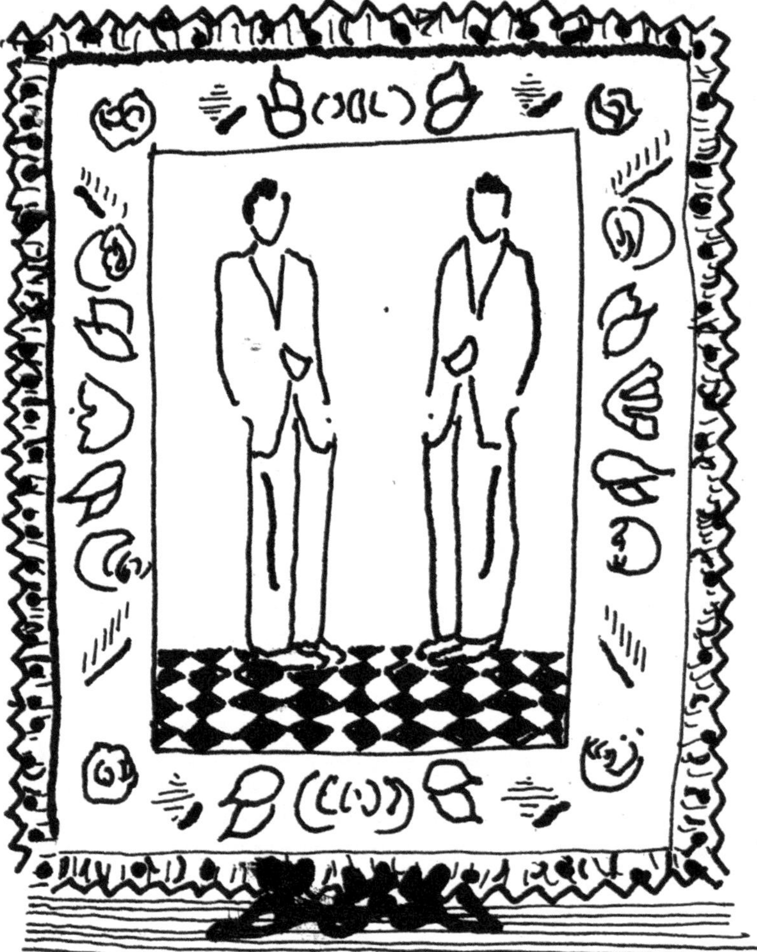

GOD
BLESS
THIS
HOUSE

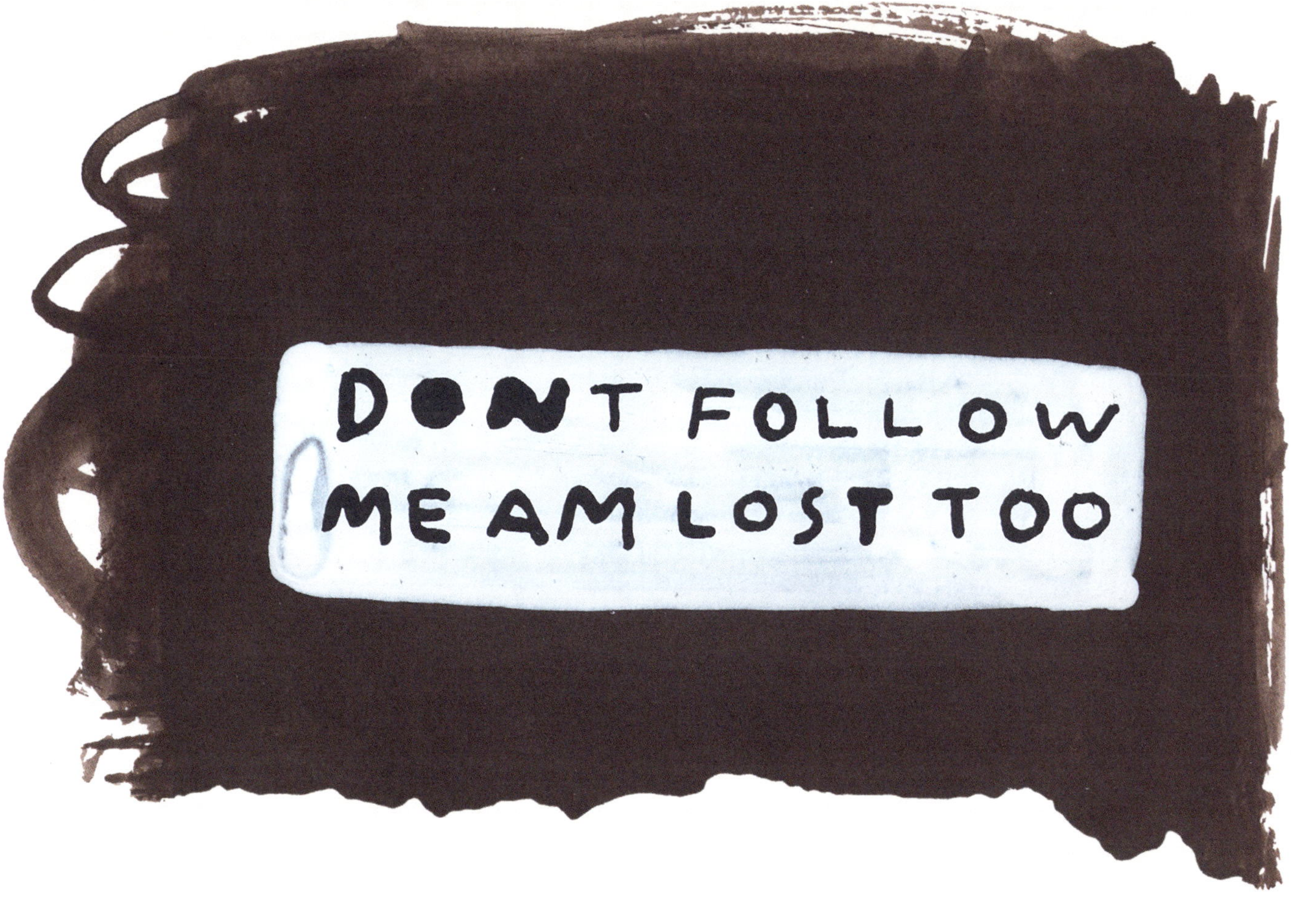

DONT FOLLOW
ME AM LOST TOO

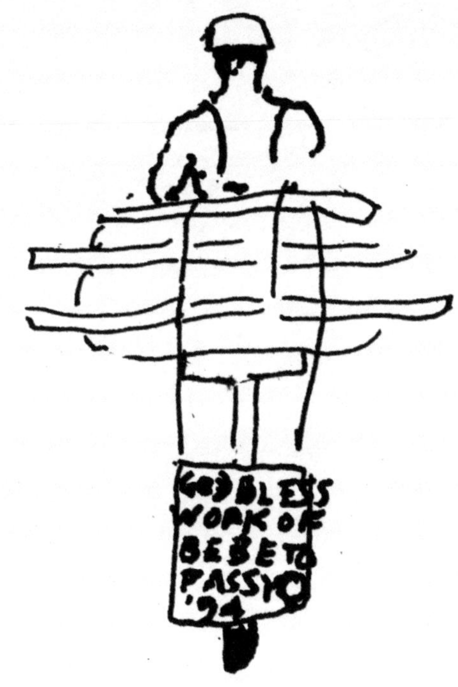
GOD BLESS
WORK OF
BEBETO
PASSYO
'94

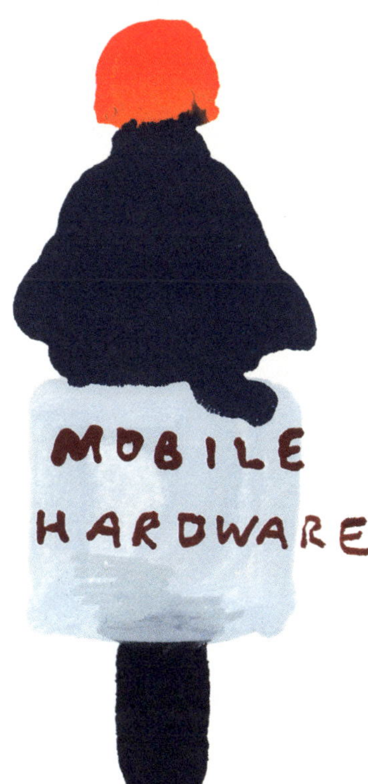
MOBILE
HARDWARE

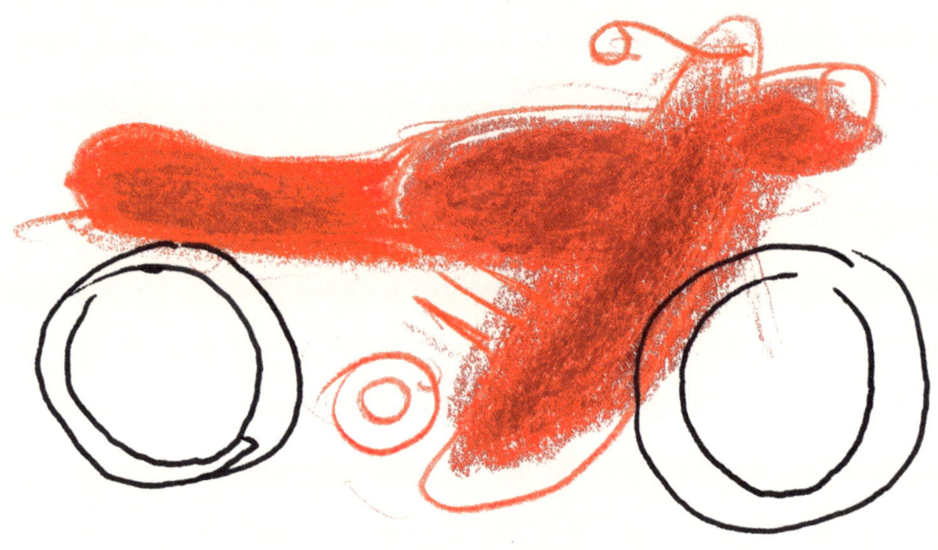

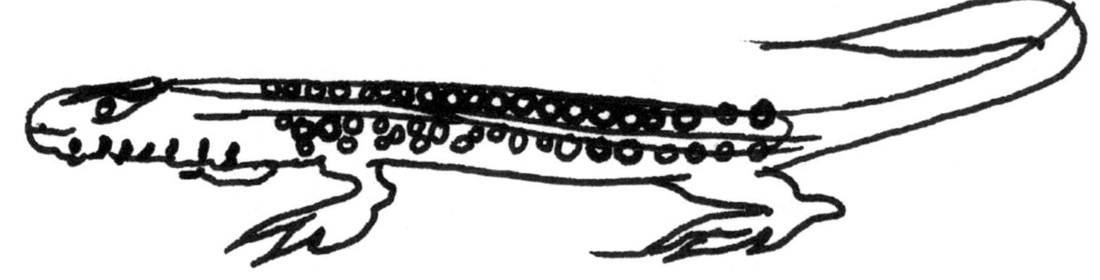

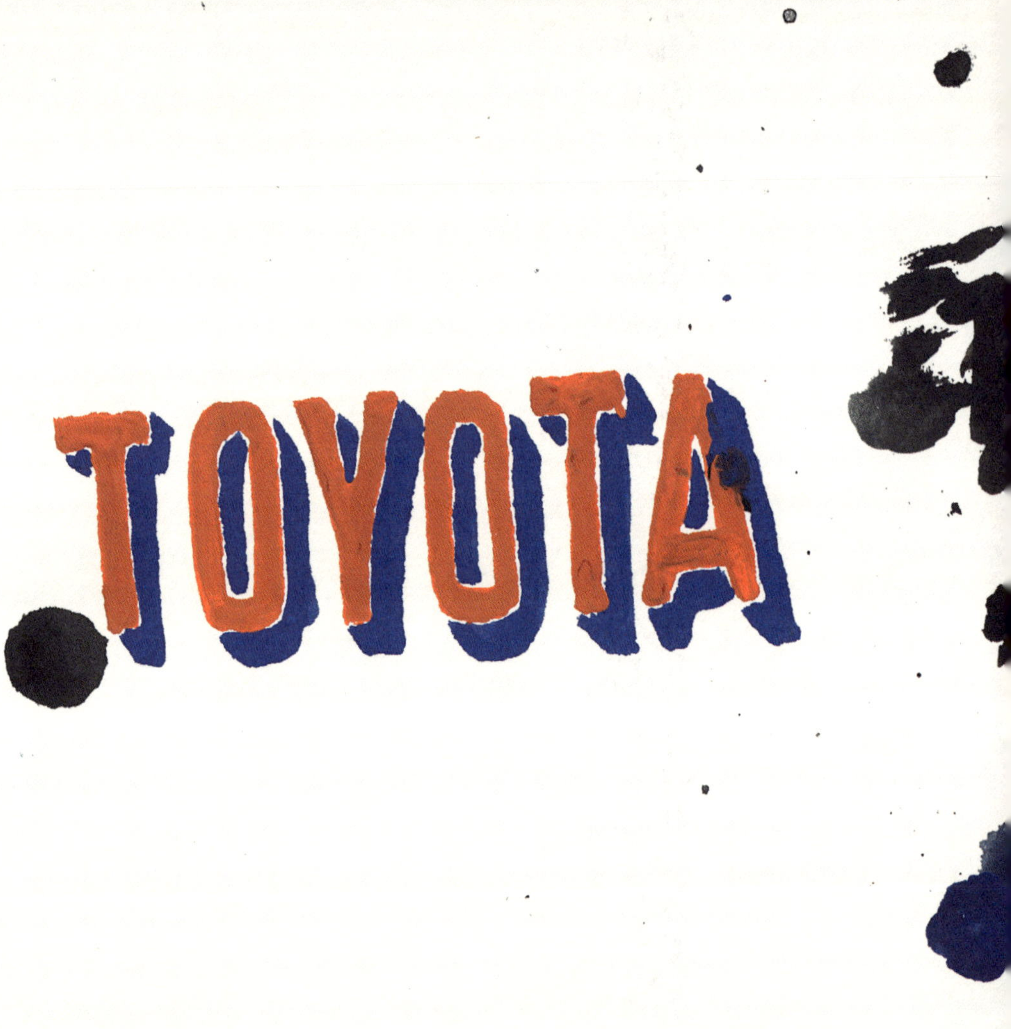

TOYOTA

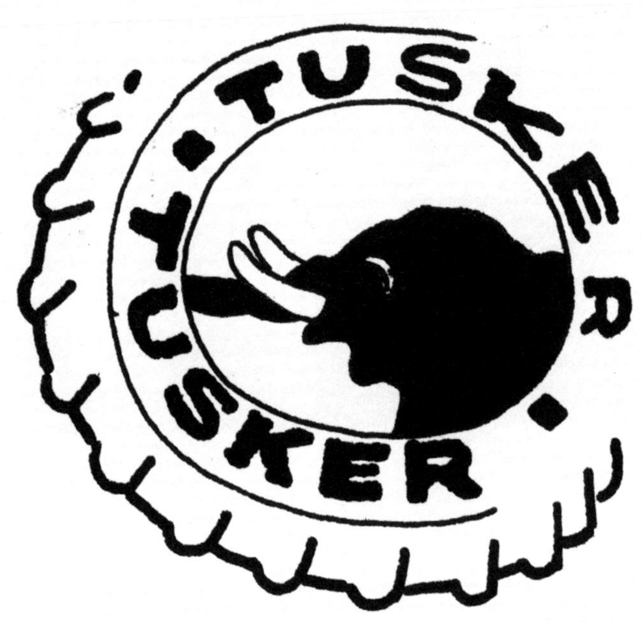

TUSKER
TUSKER

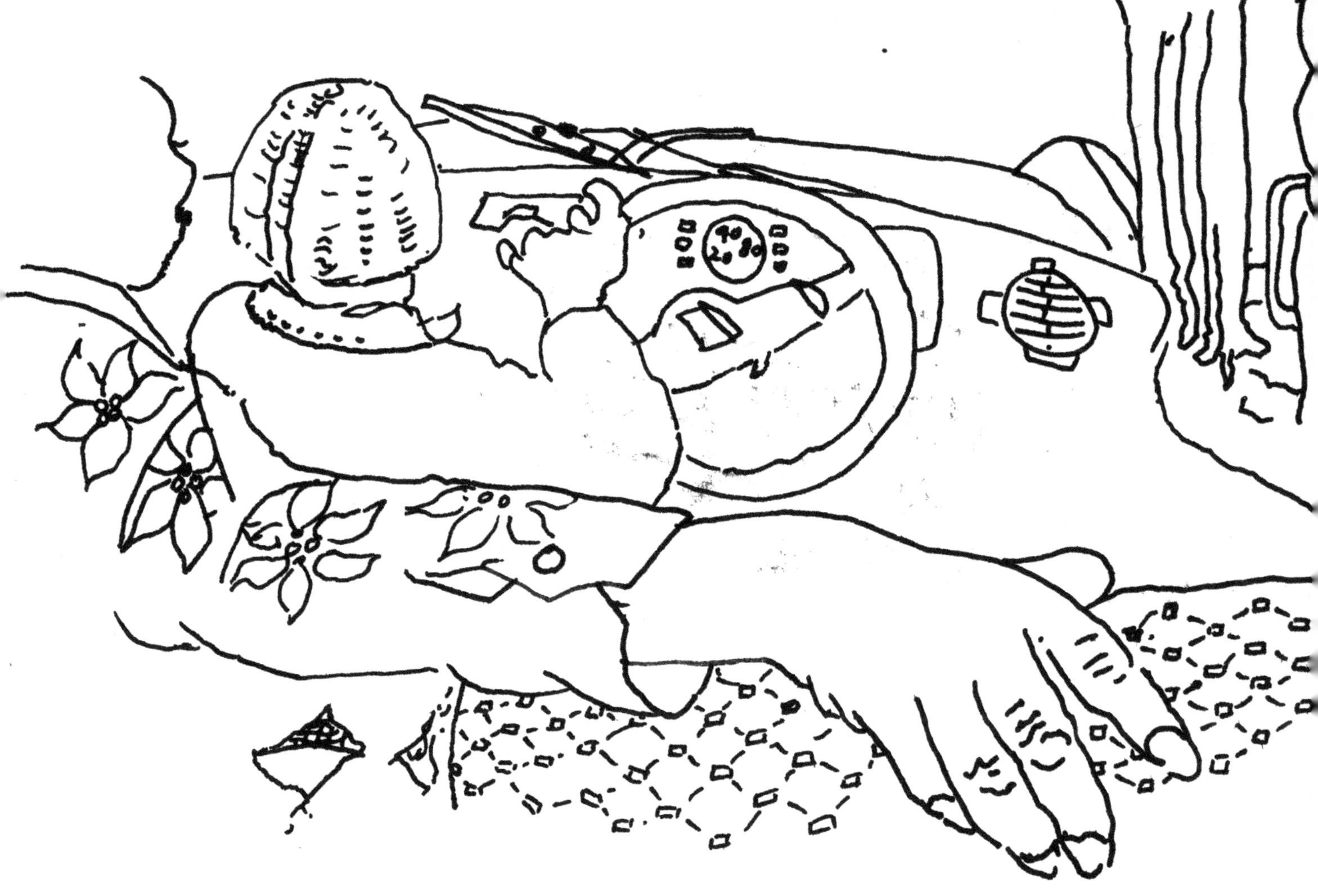

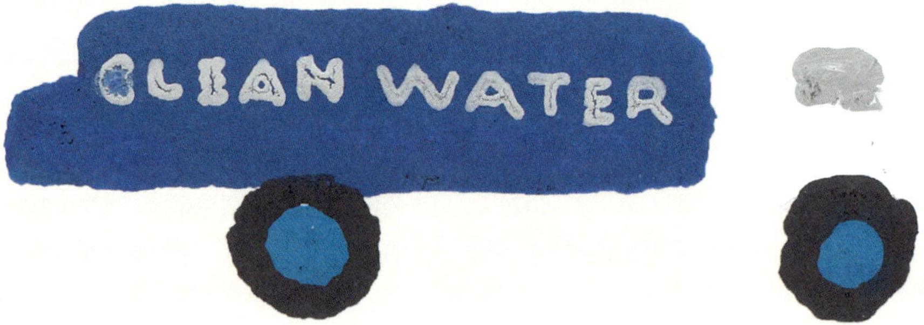

CLEAN WATER

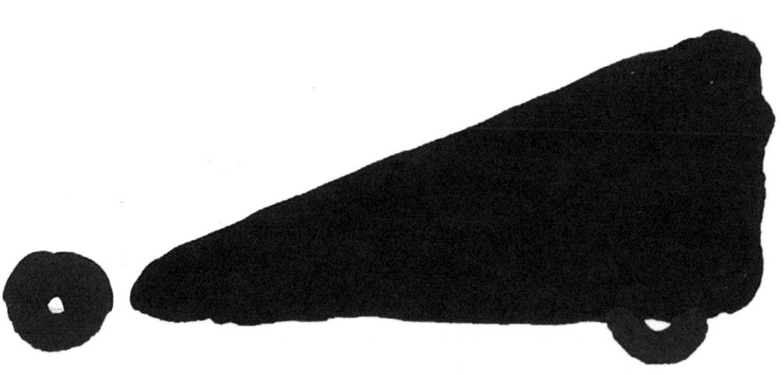

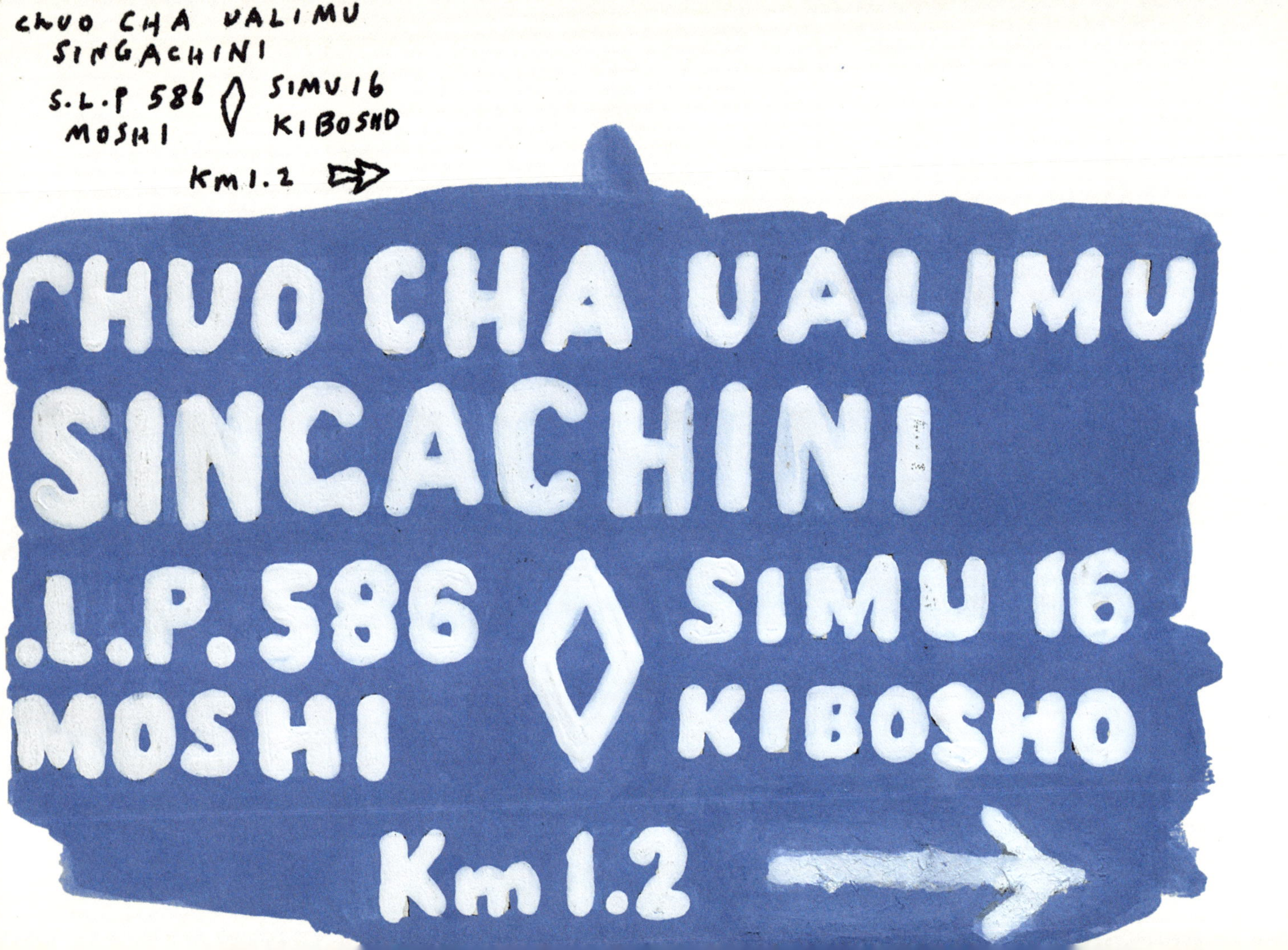

CHUO CHA UALIMU
SINGACHINI
S.L.P 586 ◊ SIMU 16
MOSHI KIBOSHO
Km 1.2 ⇨

CHUO CHA UALIMU
SINGACHINI
.L.P. 586 ◊ SIMU 16
MOSHI KIBOSHO
Km 1.2 →

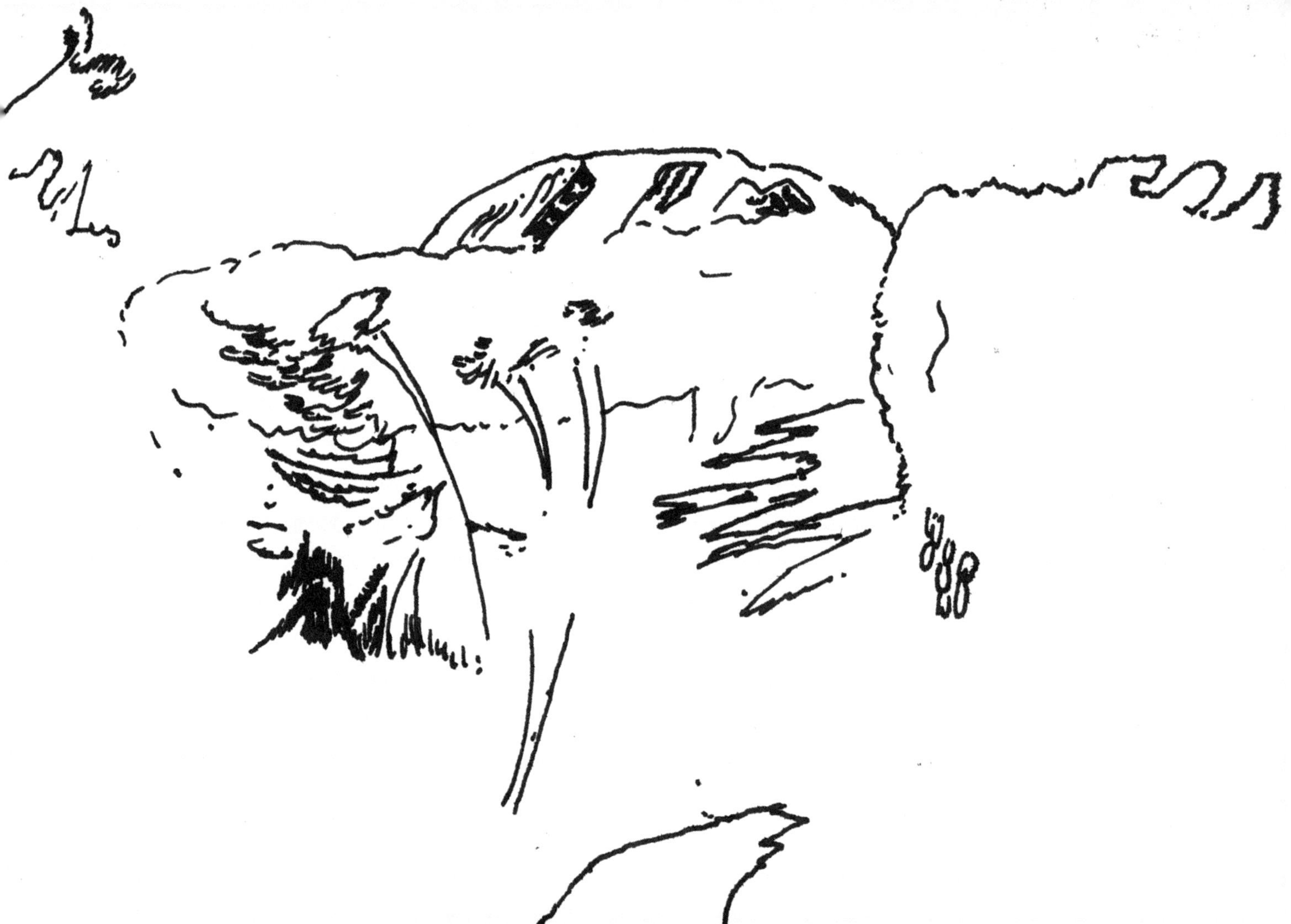

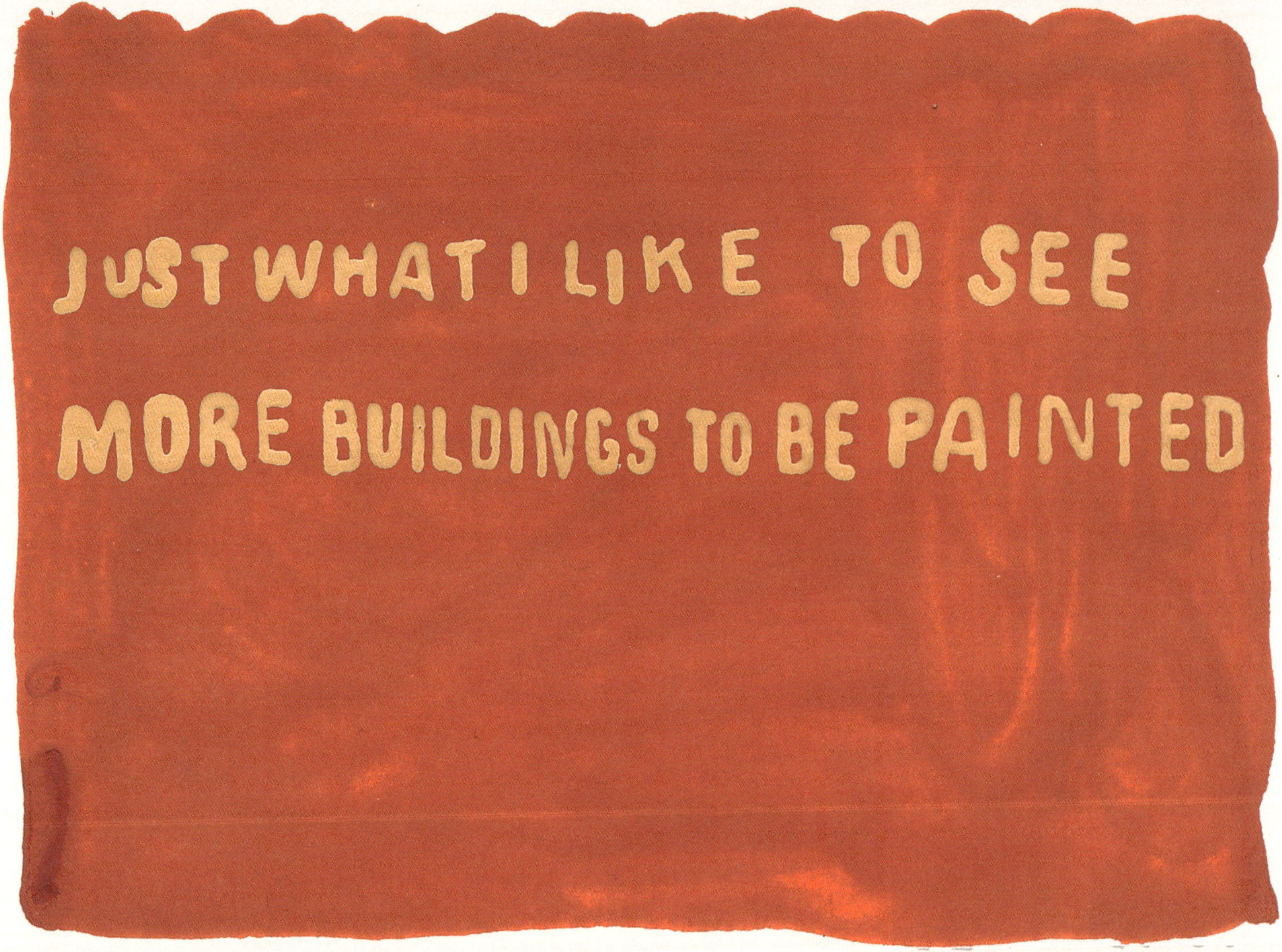

JUST WHAT I LIKE TO SEE
MORE BUILDINGS TO BE PAINTED

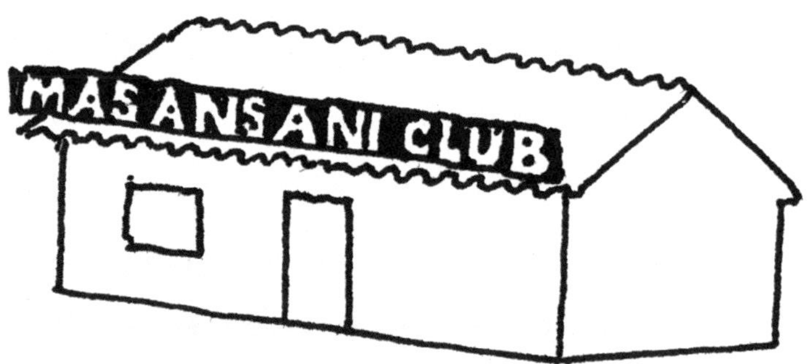
MASANSANI CLUB

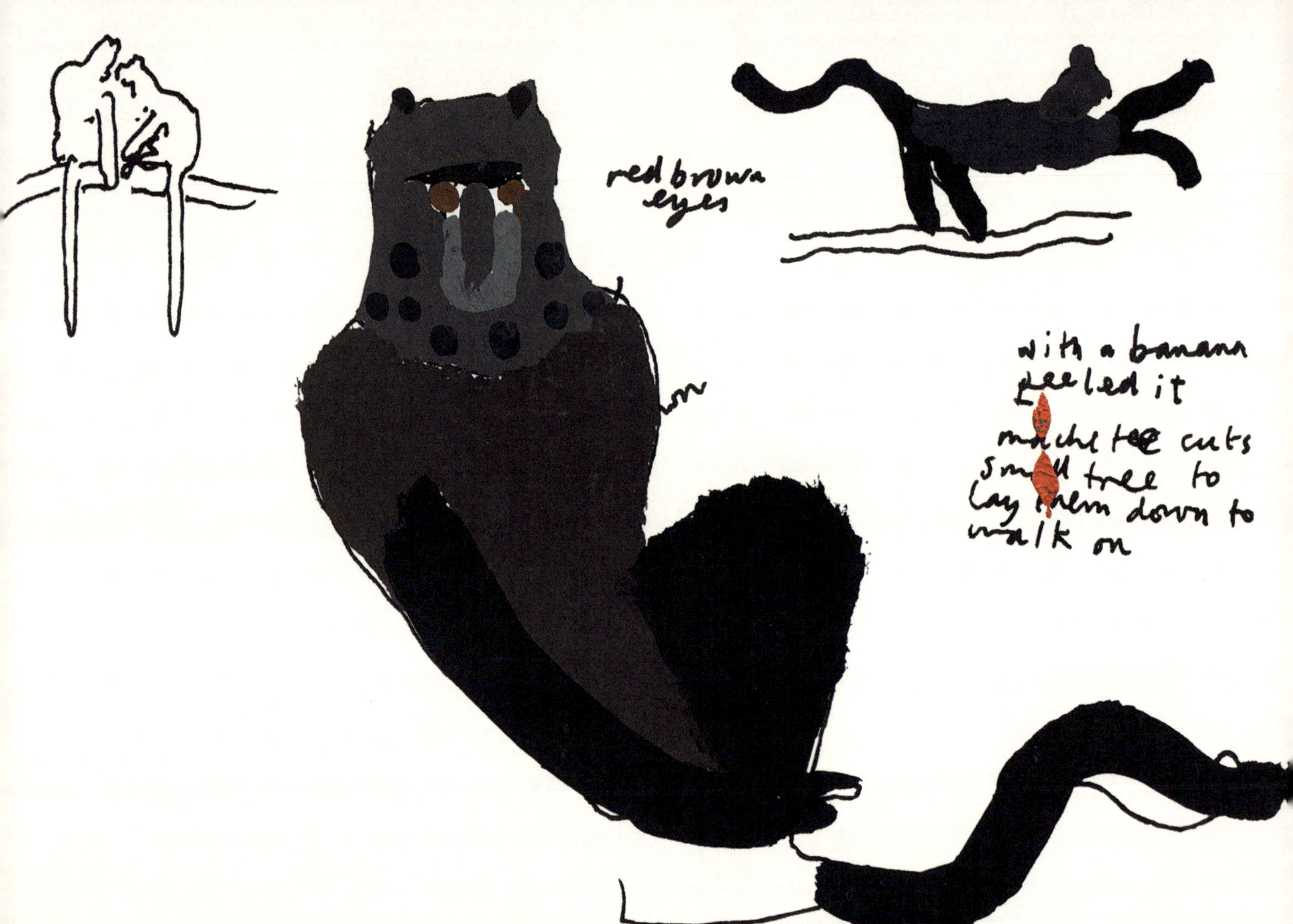
red brown
eyes
with a banana
peeled it
machetee cuts
small tree to
lay them down to
walk on

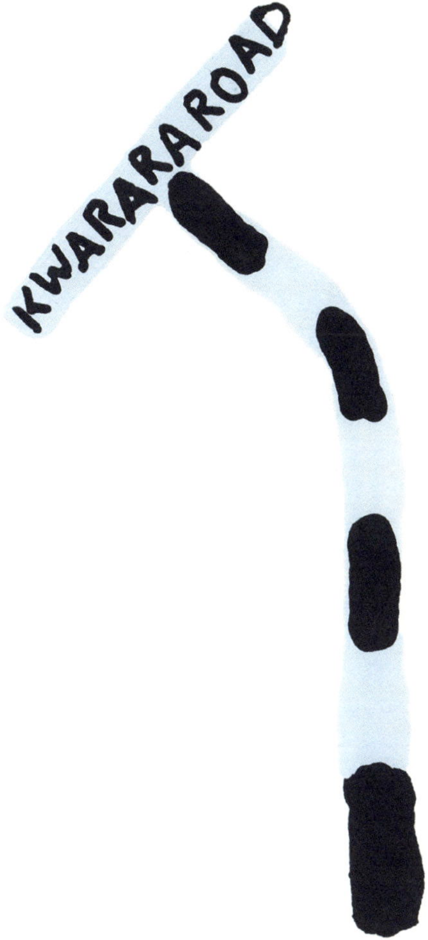

KWARARA ROAD

BOB'S WINE & SPIRITS

NJORO'S HI-TECH
HARDWARE

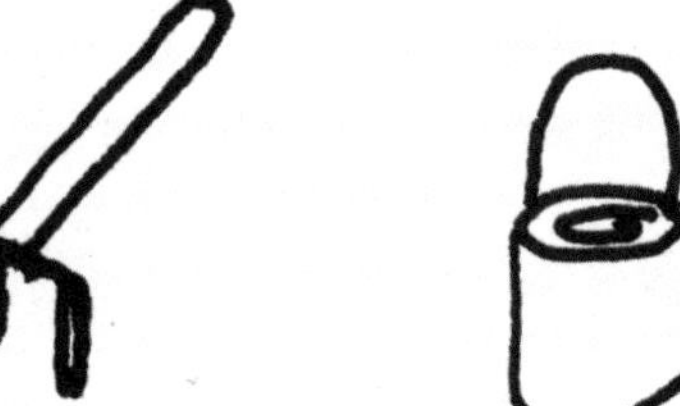

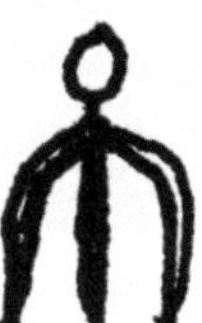

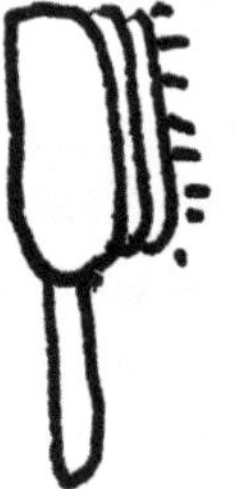

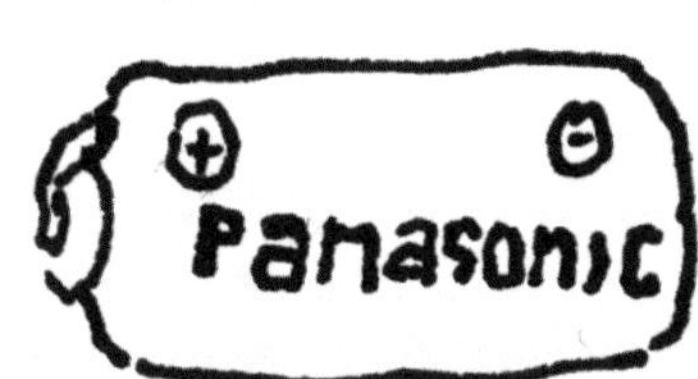

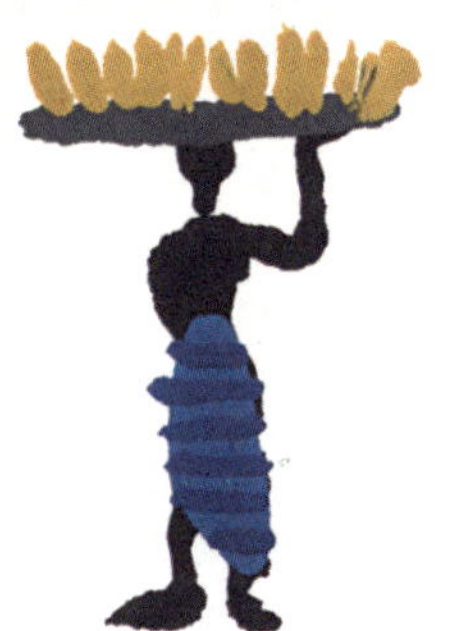

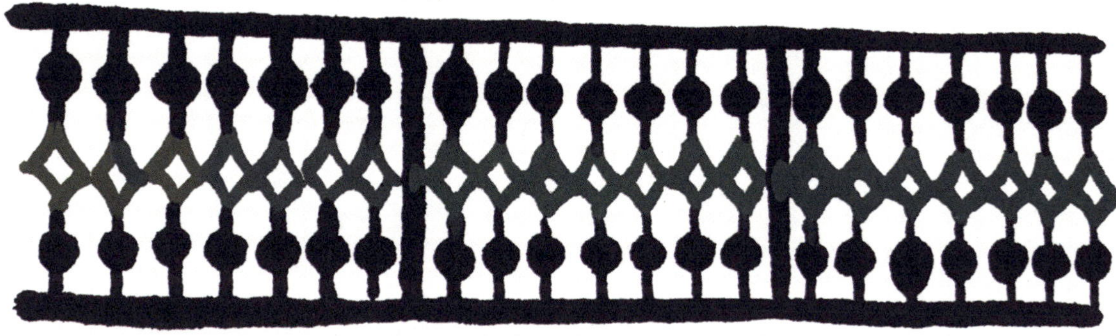

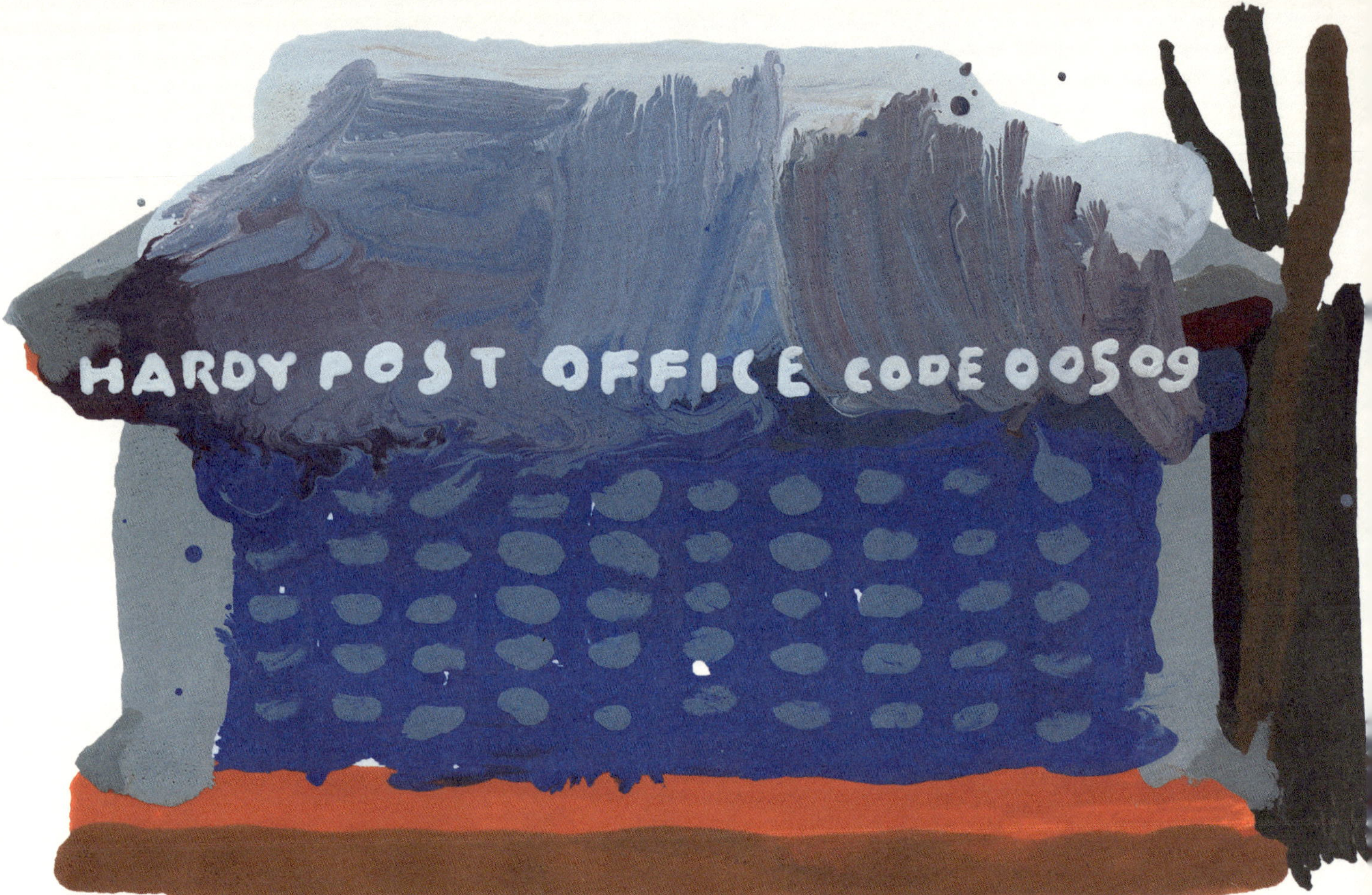

HARDY POST OFFICE CODE 00509

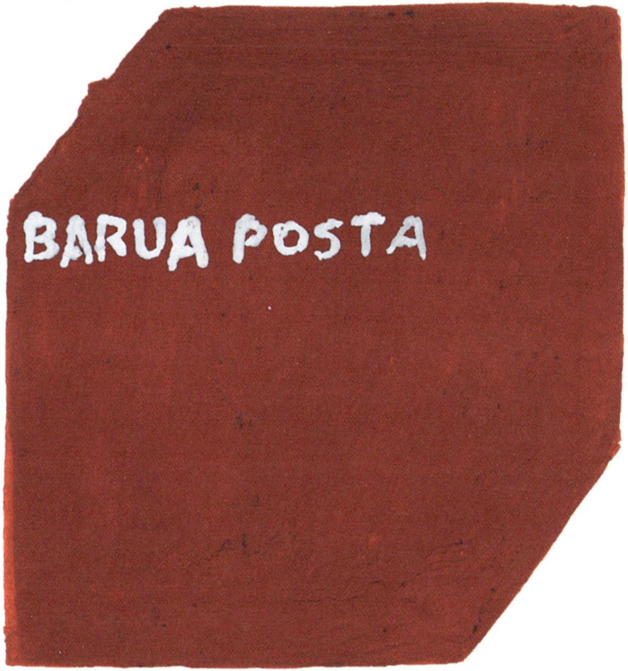

BARUA POSTA

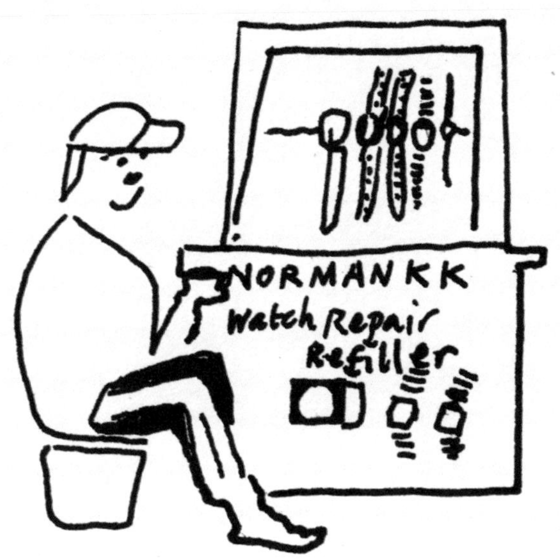
NORMAN KK
Watch Repair
Refiller

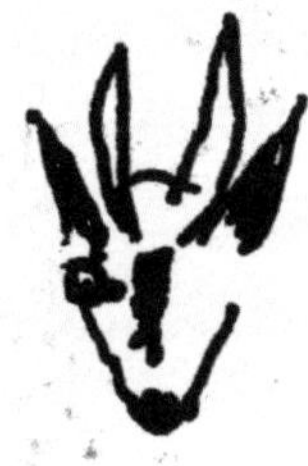

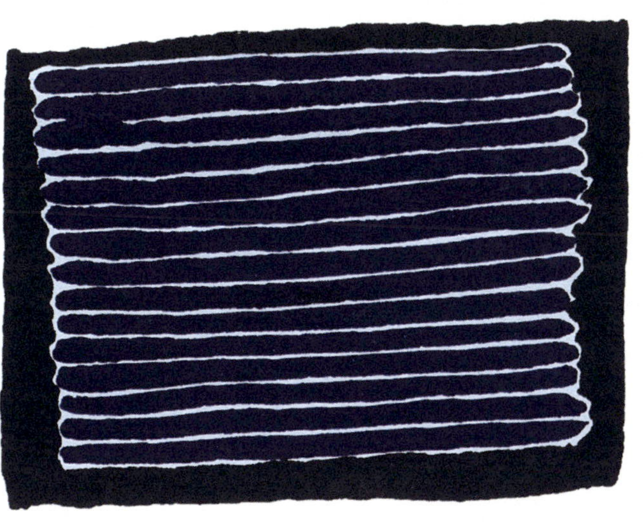

THE BIG PUNISHER SHOESHINE

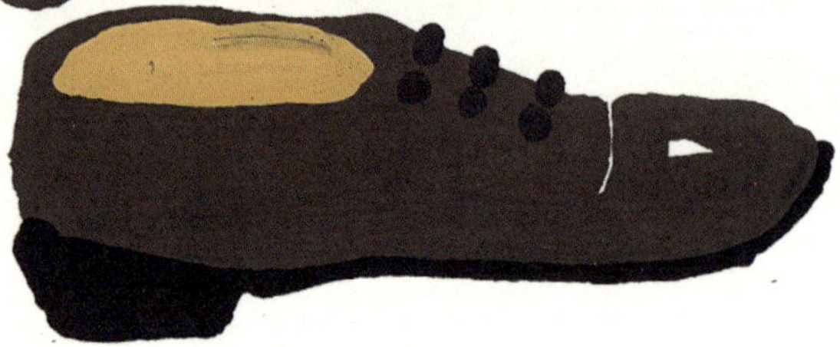

VICTORY TINSMITIH

LAND NOT
FOR SALE

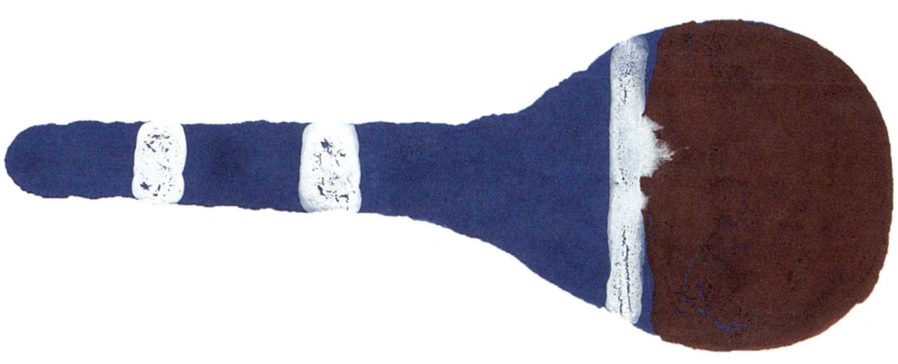

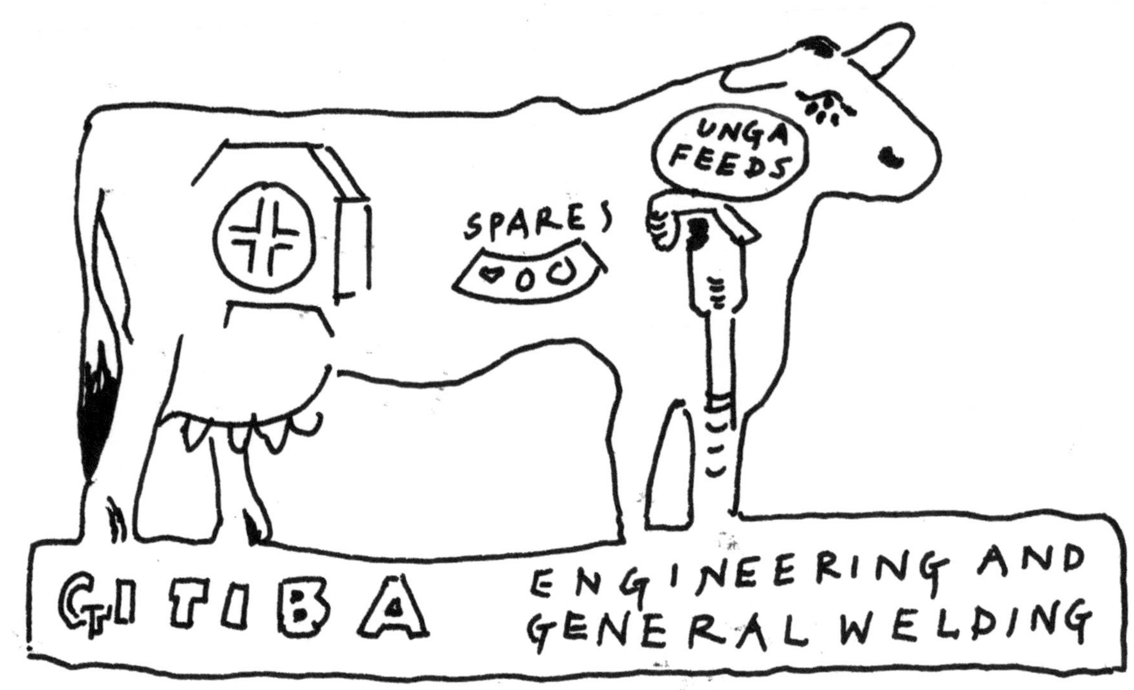
UNGA FEEDS
SPARES
CITIBA
ENGINEERING AND GENERAL WELDING

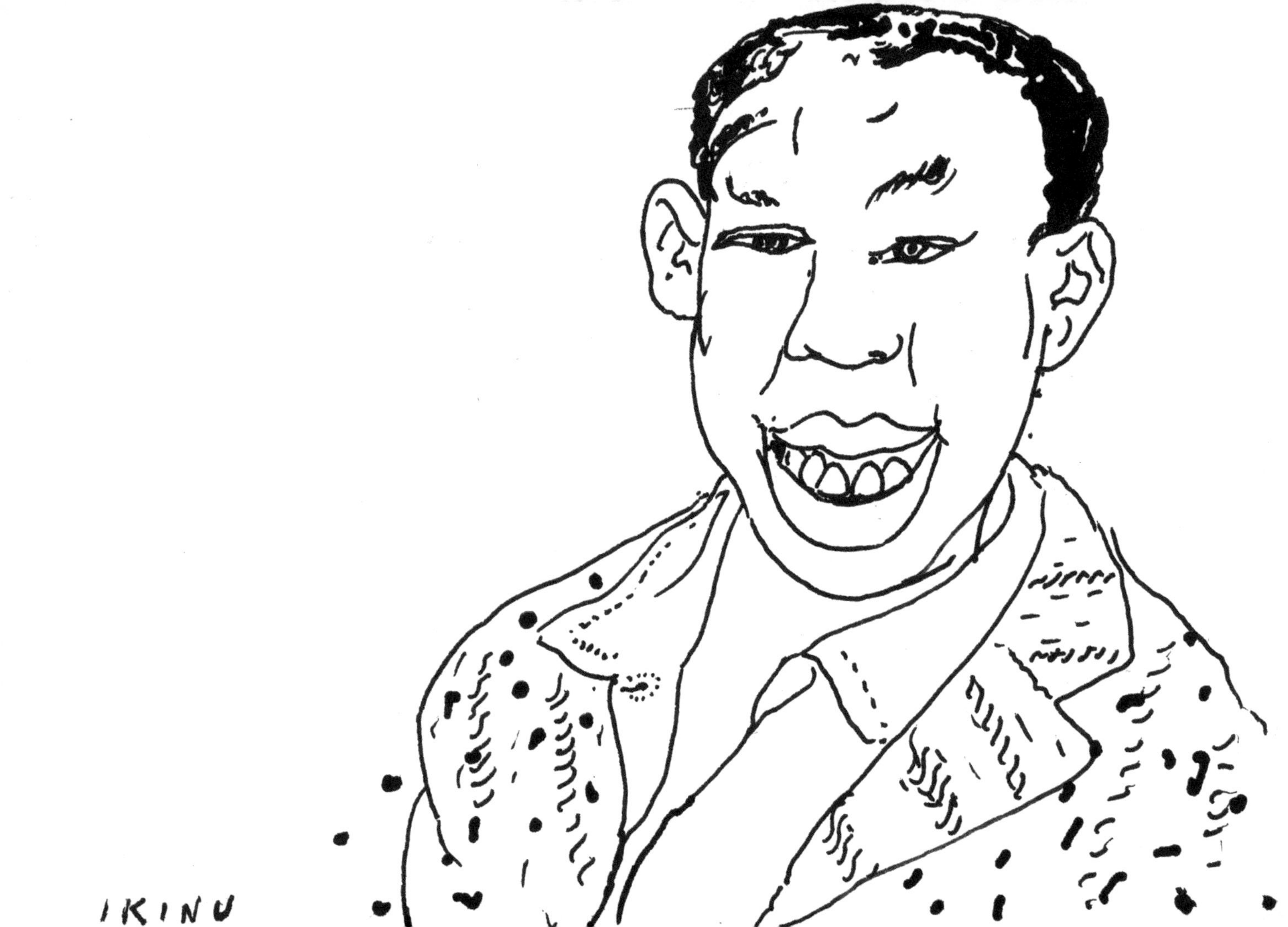
IKINU

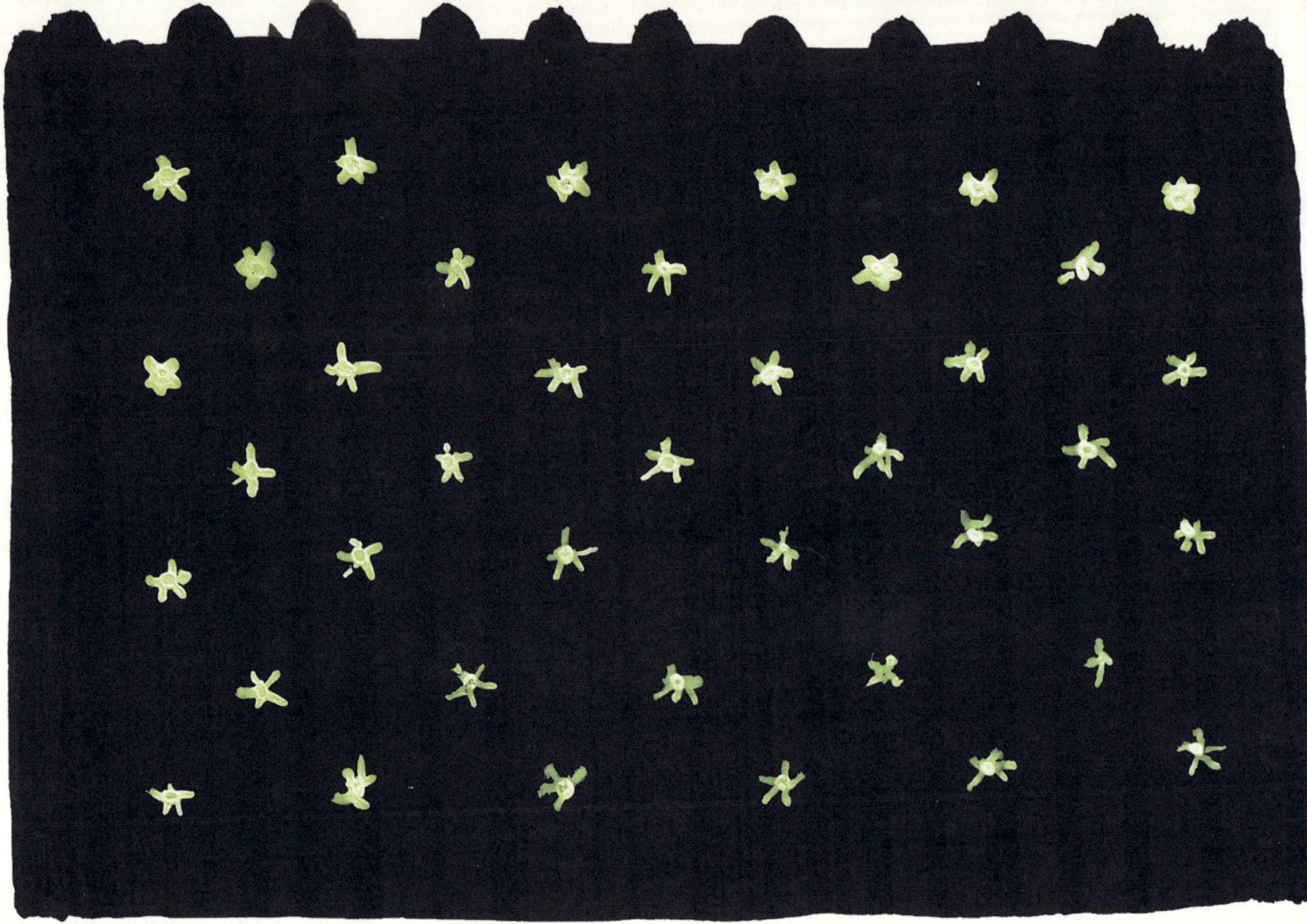

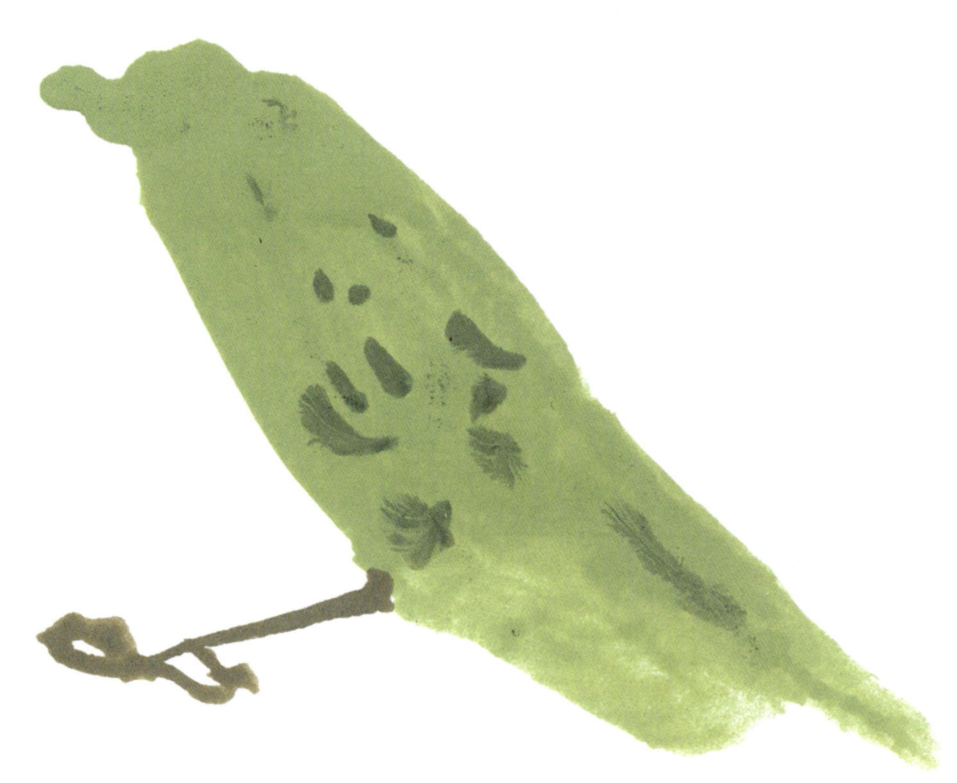

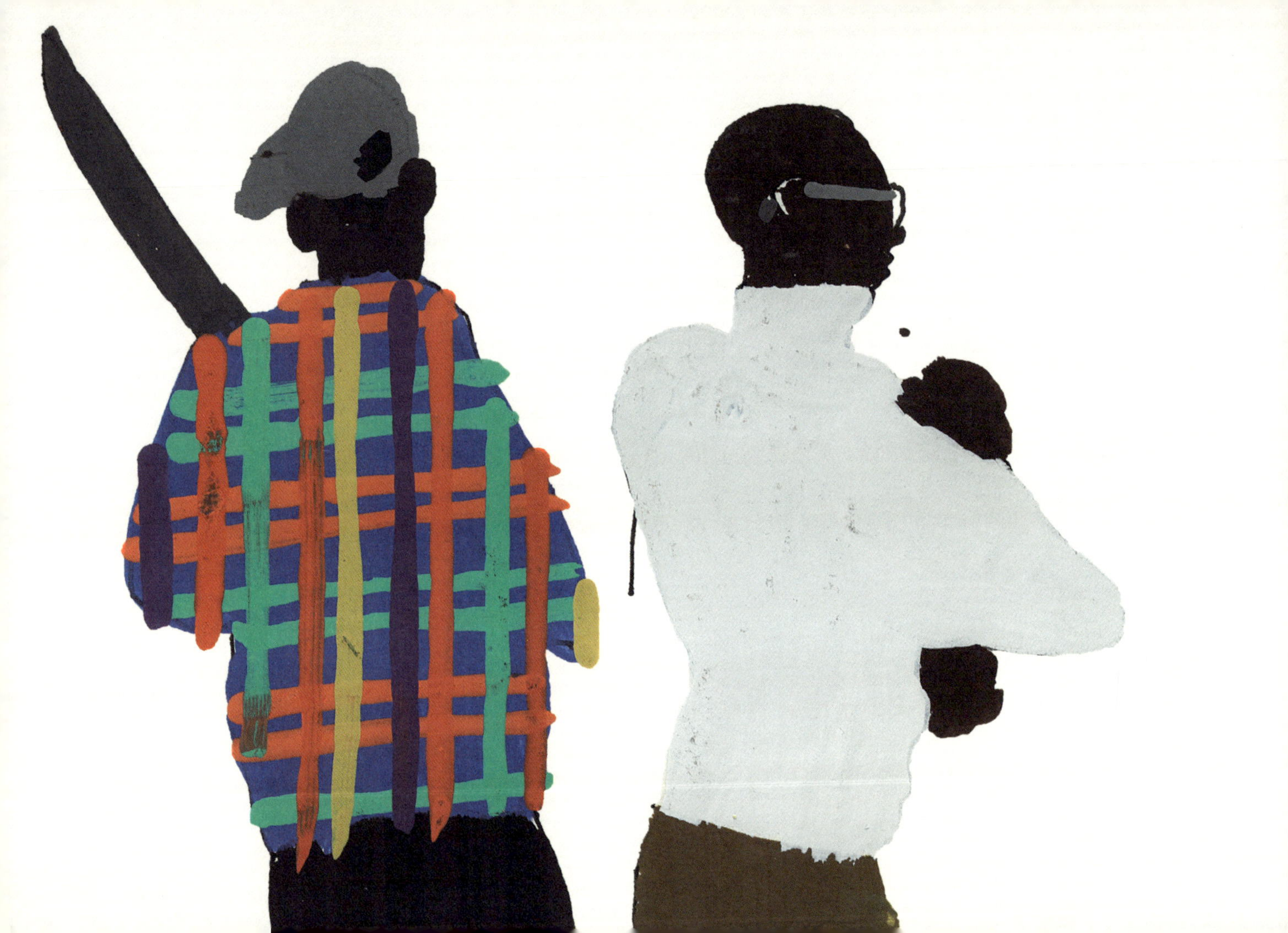

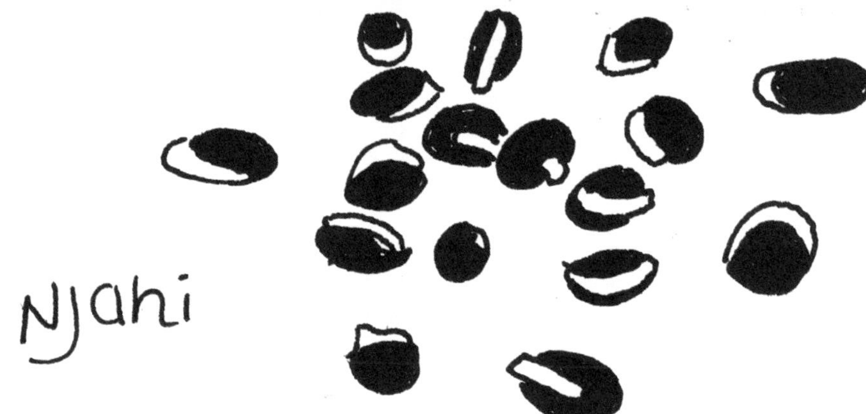

kikuyu ceremonial bean

OBEY
YOUR
THIRST

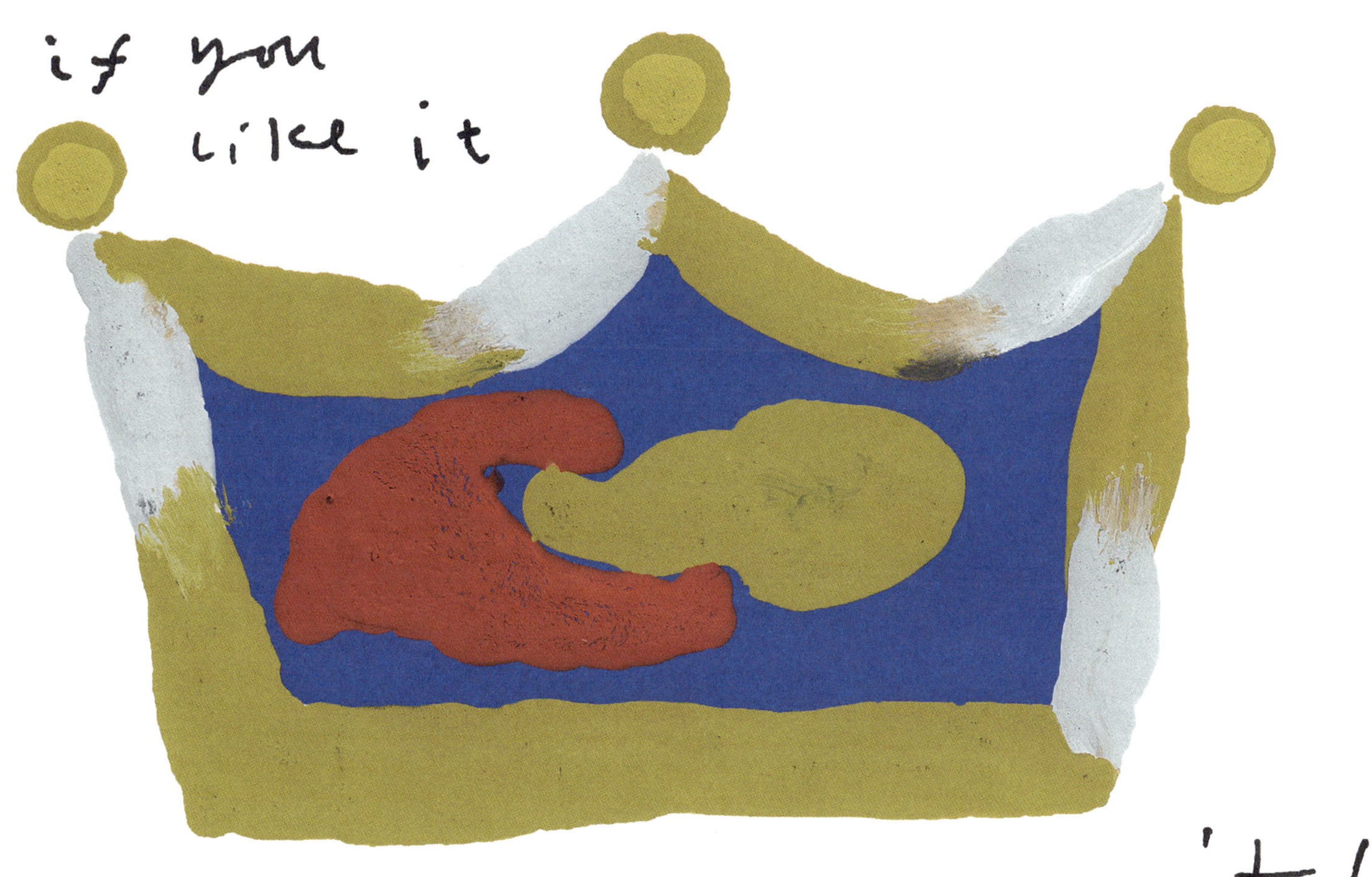
if you
like it
it!

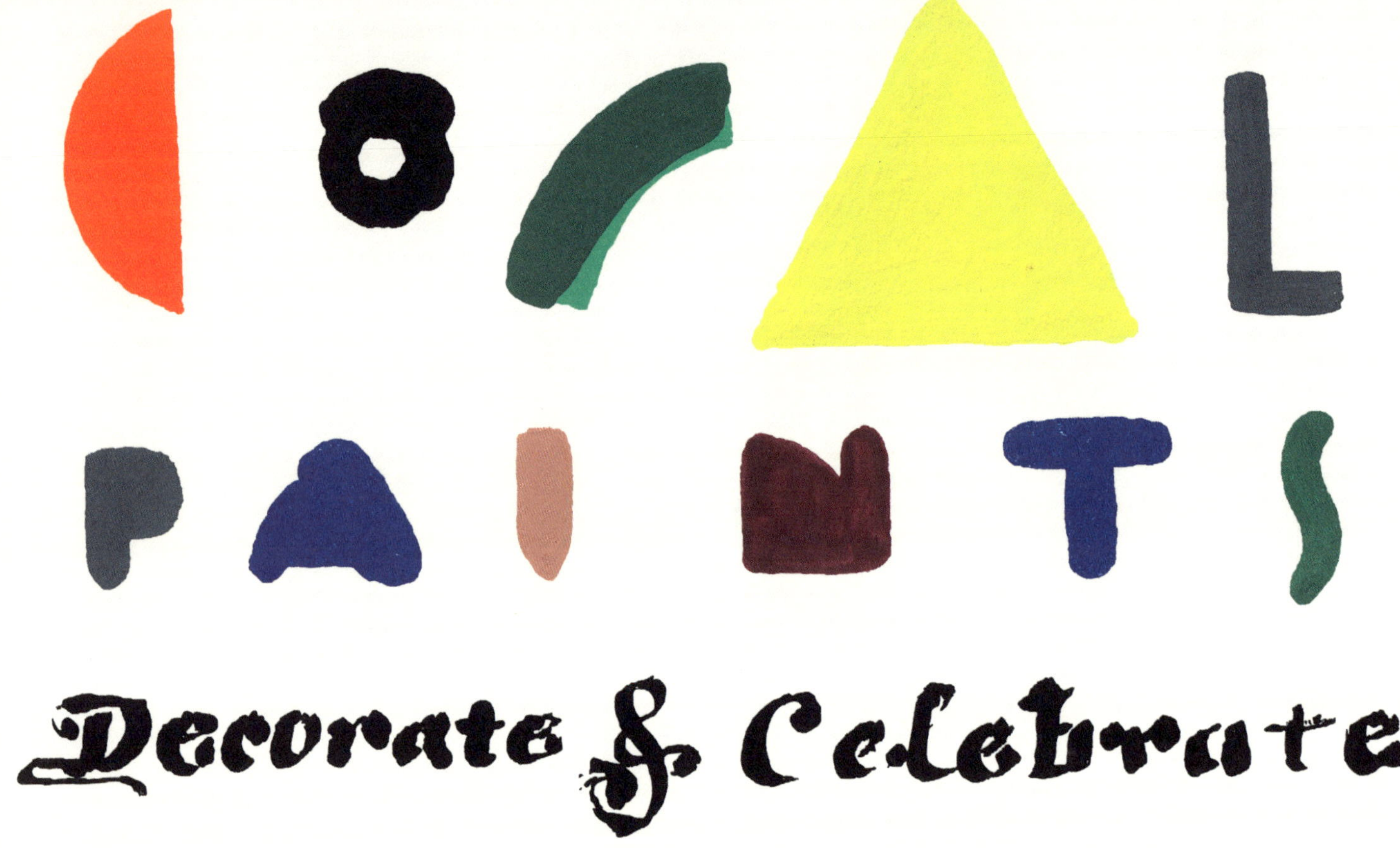
PAINTS
Decorate & Celebrate

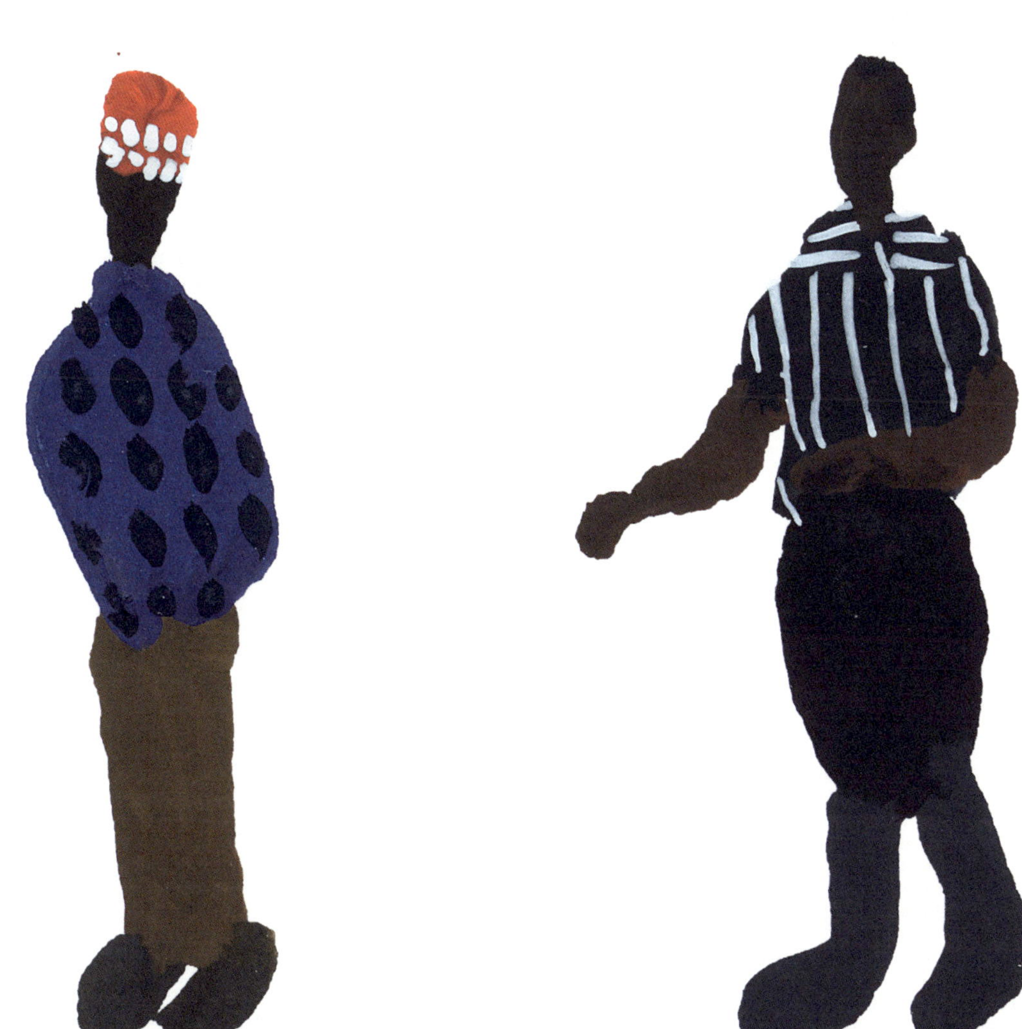

AN ASTROLOGER

•IMPOTENCE etc

•BROKEN MARRIAGE

•BAD OMEN •LOST LOVER

MOST COMPOTENT • ON ALL

DOMESTIC PROBLEMS IN

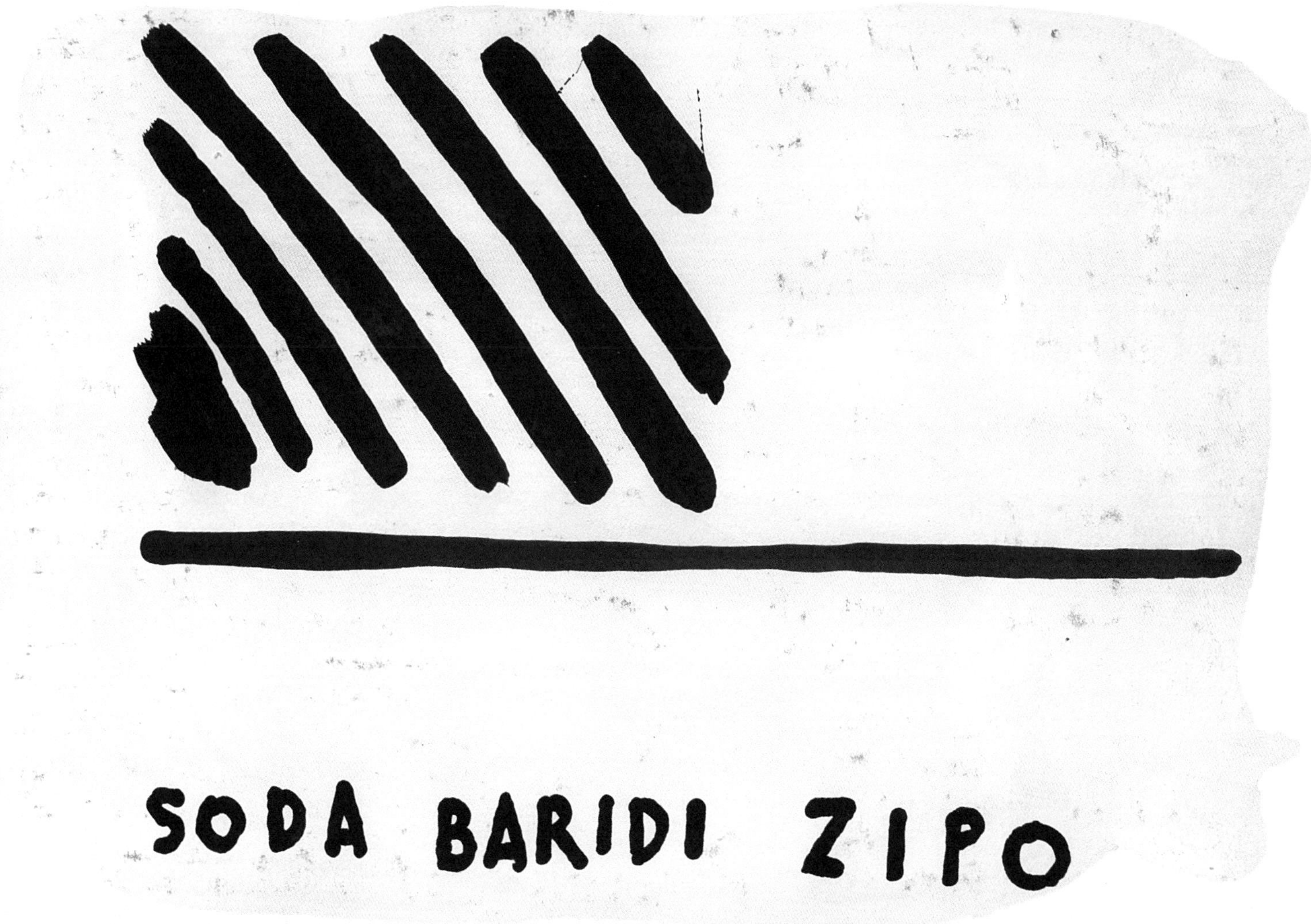

SODA BARIDI ZIPO

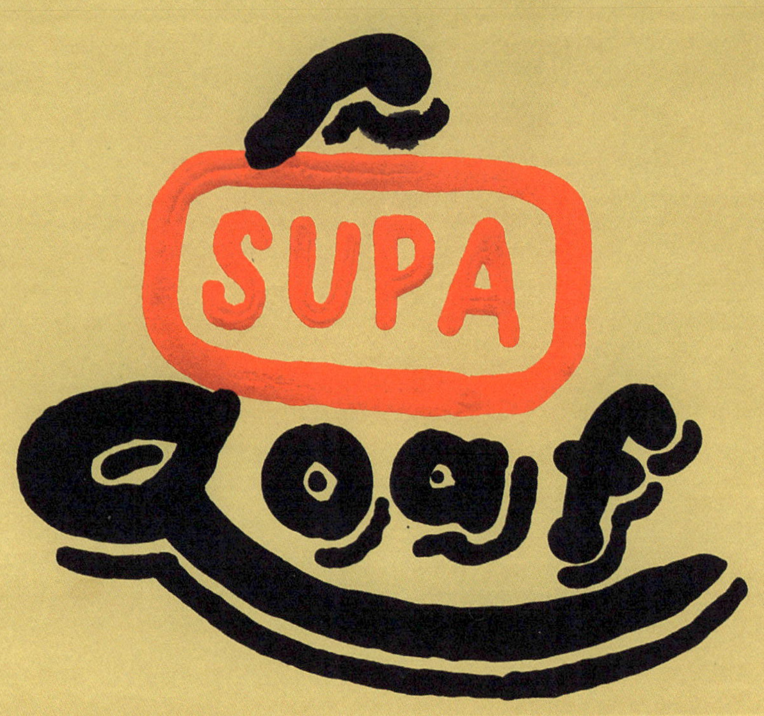
SUPA

ATTENTION!!

GET RID OF BED BUGS FOREVER

CALL 0724 58

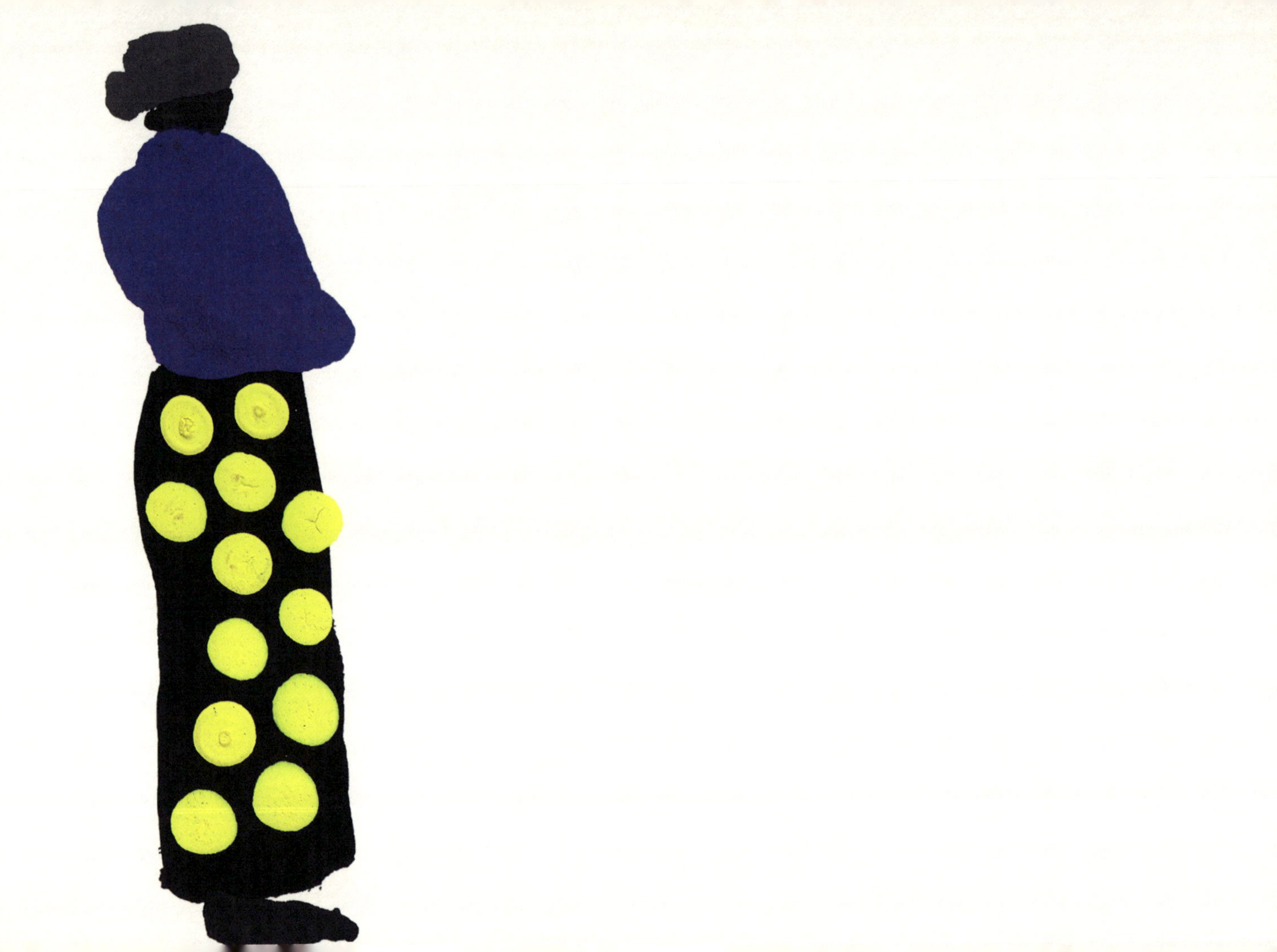

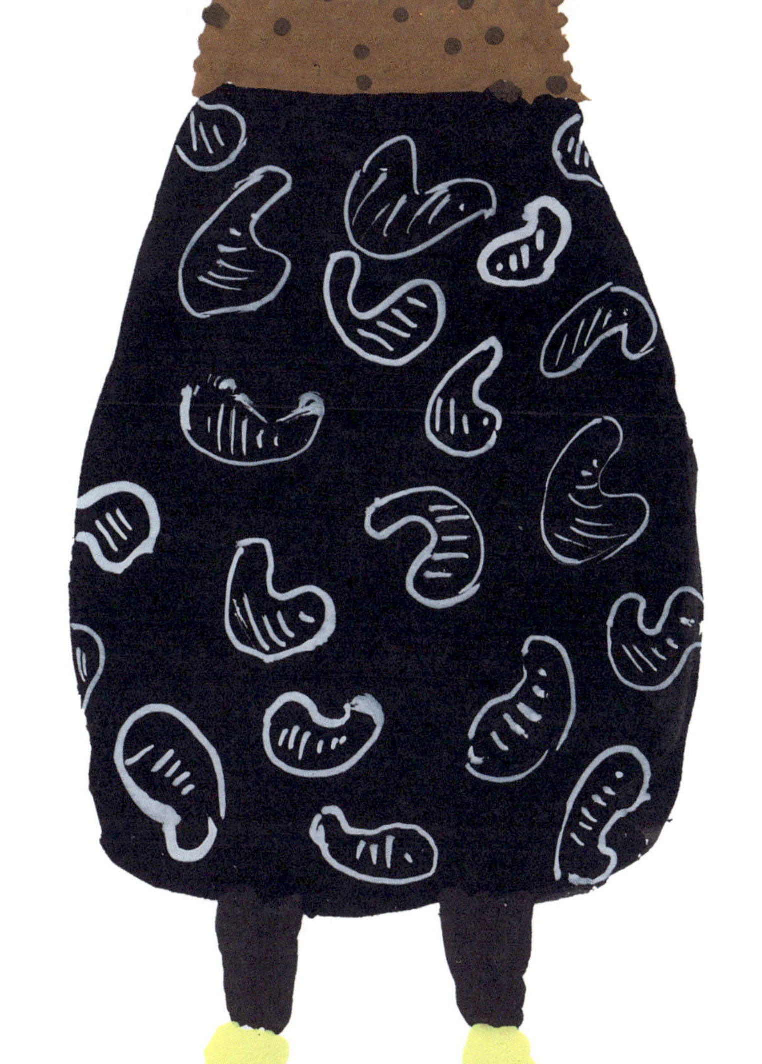

EXCELLENT SOFA SETS

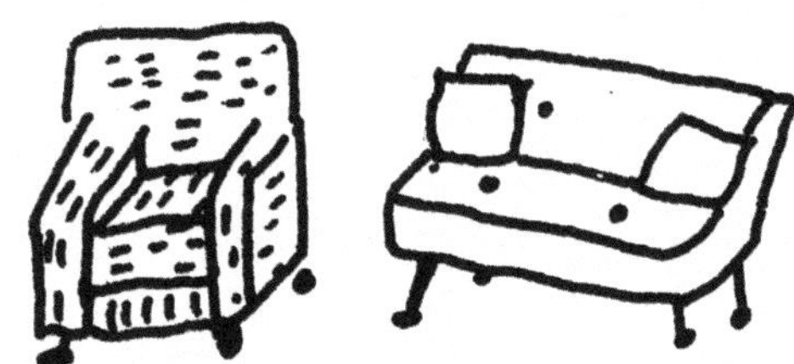

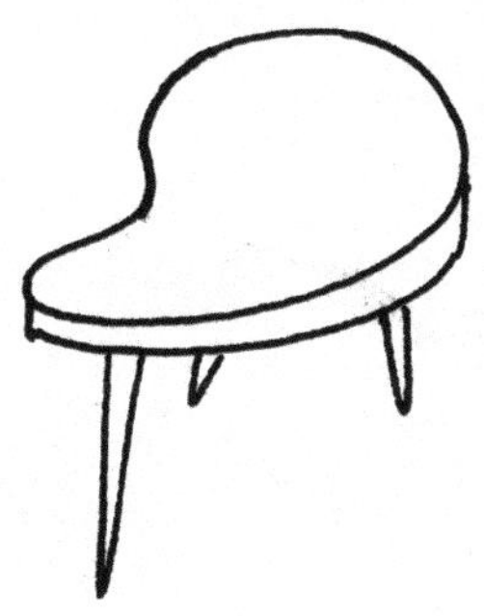

because cows milk too fatty and their digestion is not very good. It took Daphne several years to get mixture right 'trial and error' as keeper said - during which time they lost a lot of baby elephants.. Off in the distance was (? Rift Valley) national park and through binocs saw zebra, impala (anyway something deer-like w blackish heads, quite big) and one buffalo. On the walk back to the main road three young warthogs crossed our path. A bit nearer gate we saw more, one was kneeling on its front knees, snuffling. As the rest came and joined him, one was swivelling in the air. They are most elegant creatures but would not win beauty competitions.
on walk home from bus stop saw sunbird, collared flycatcher and a small sparrow like bird marked like a snipe but duller. Over main gate, in acacia tree, are several sparrow-weavers nests which the weavers are building, straw by straw. They hang from dangling branches - the nests - you wonder how they get the first straws to grip.

It doesn't look
like much now
but wait til
its painted

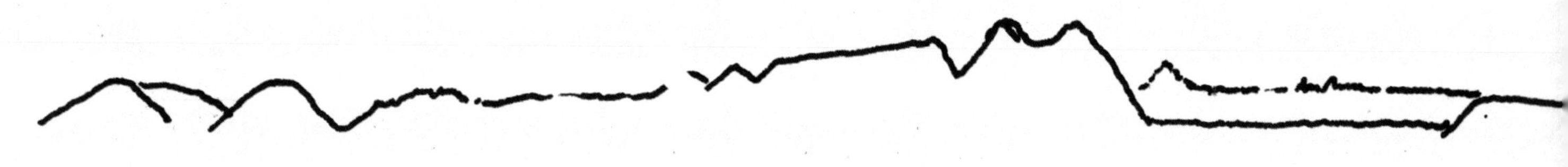

LAKE ELMENTEITA

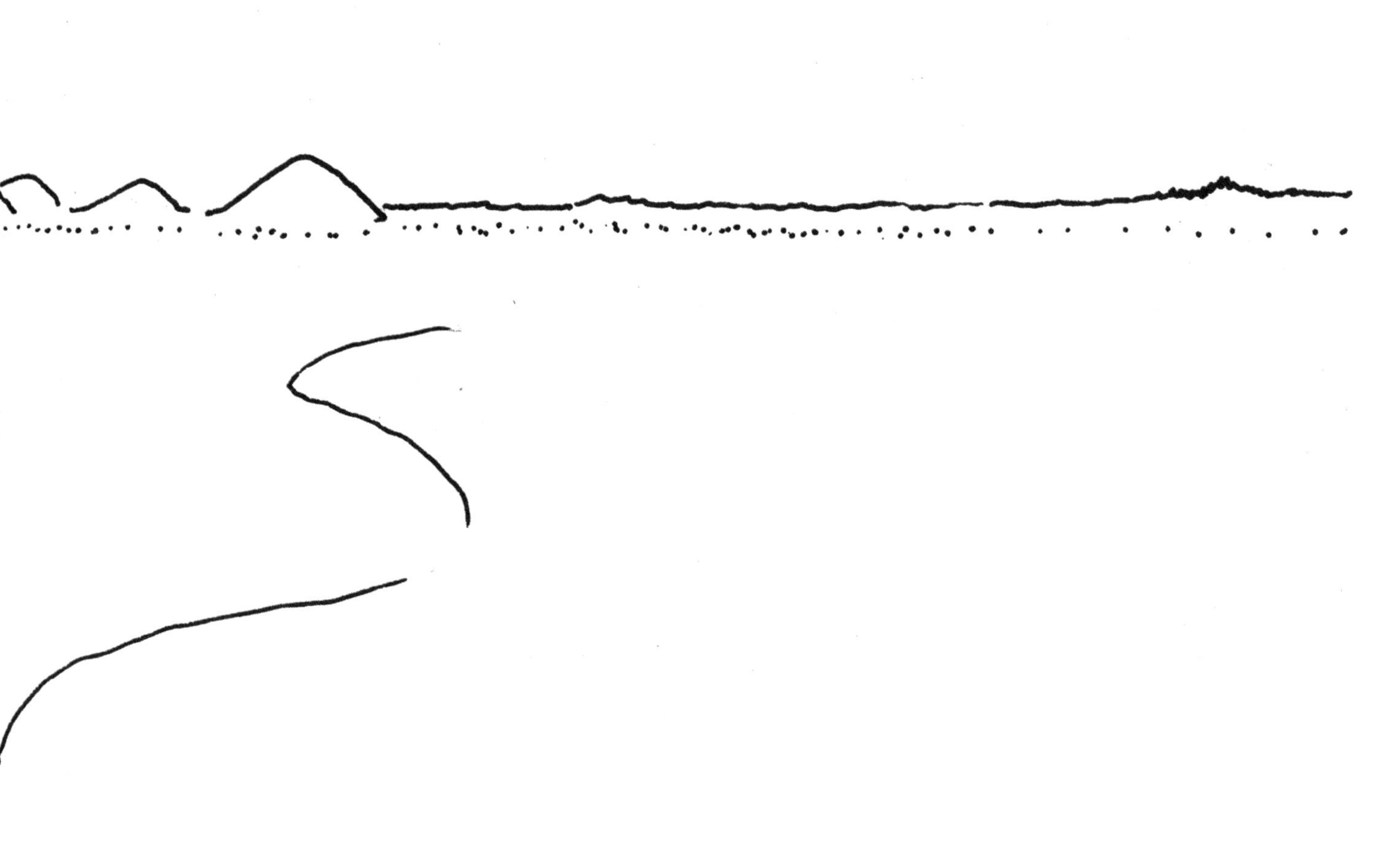

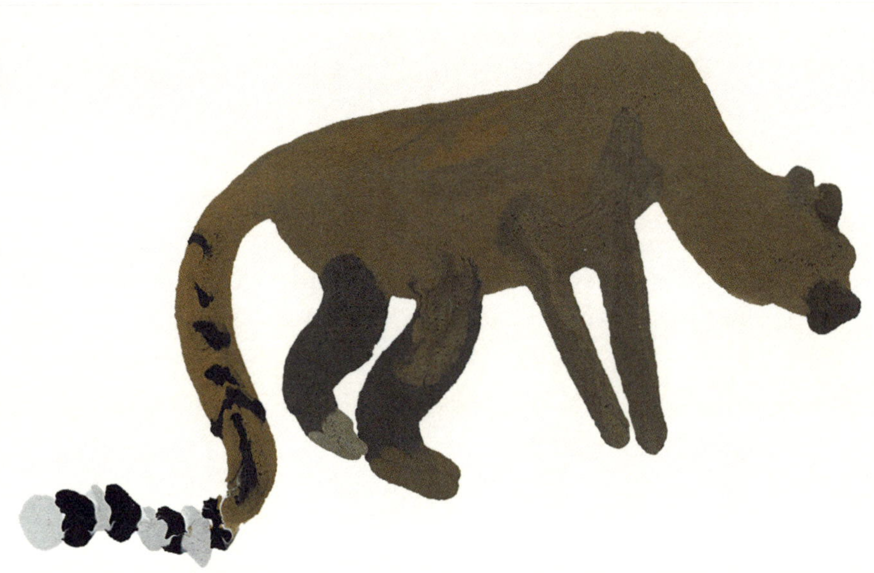

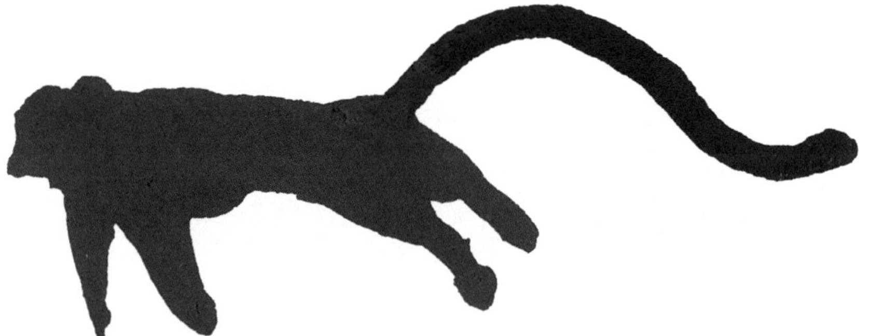

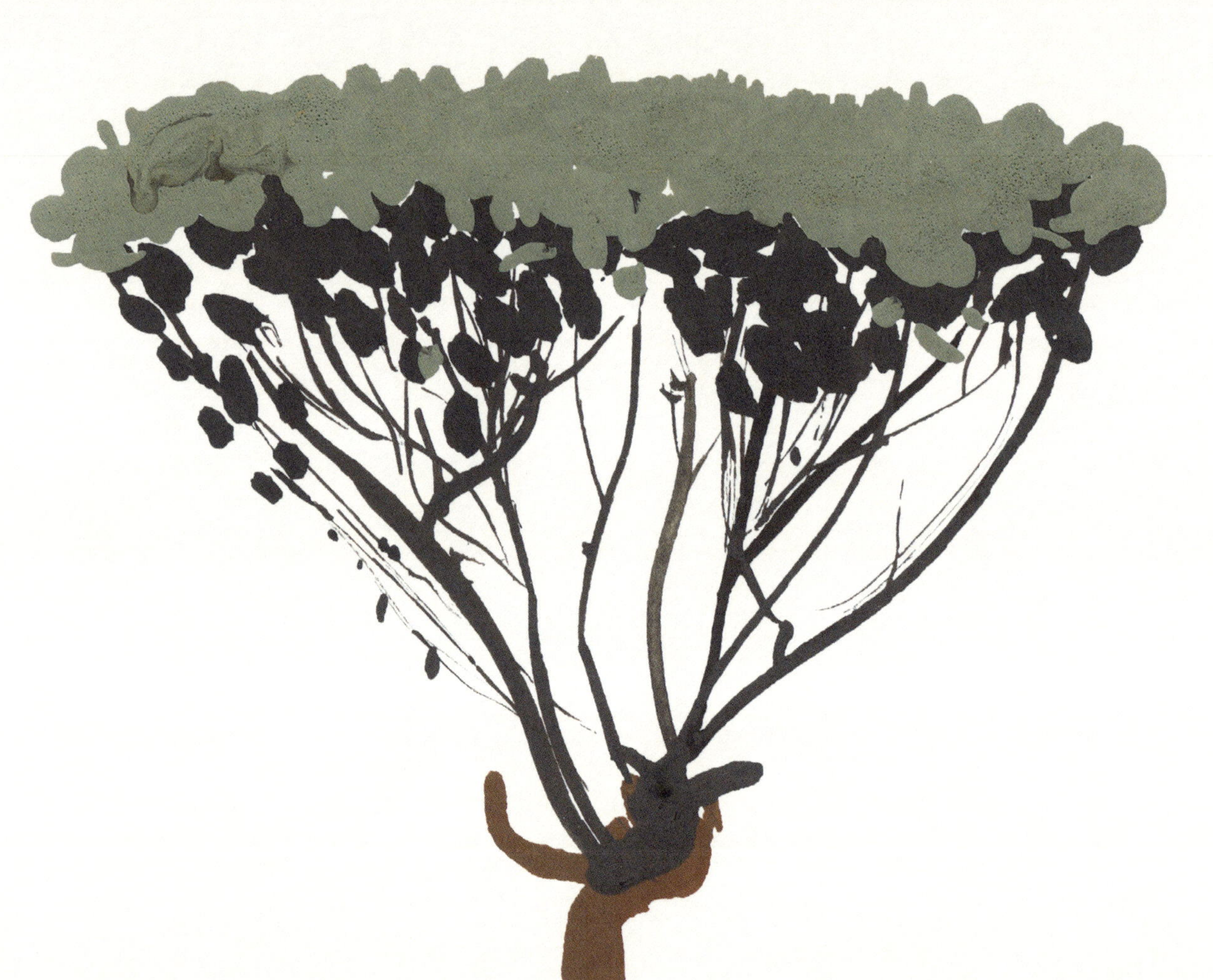

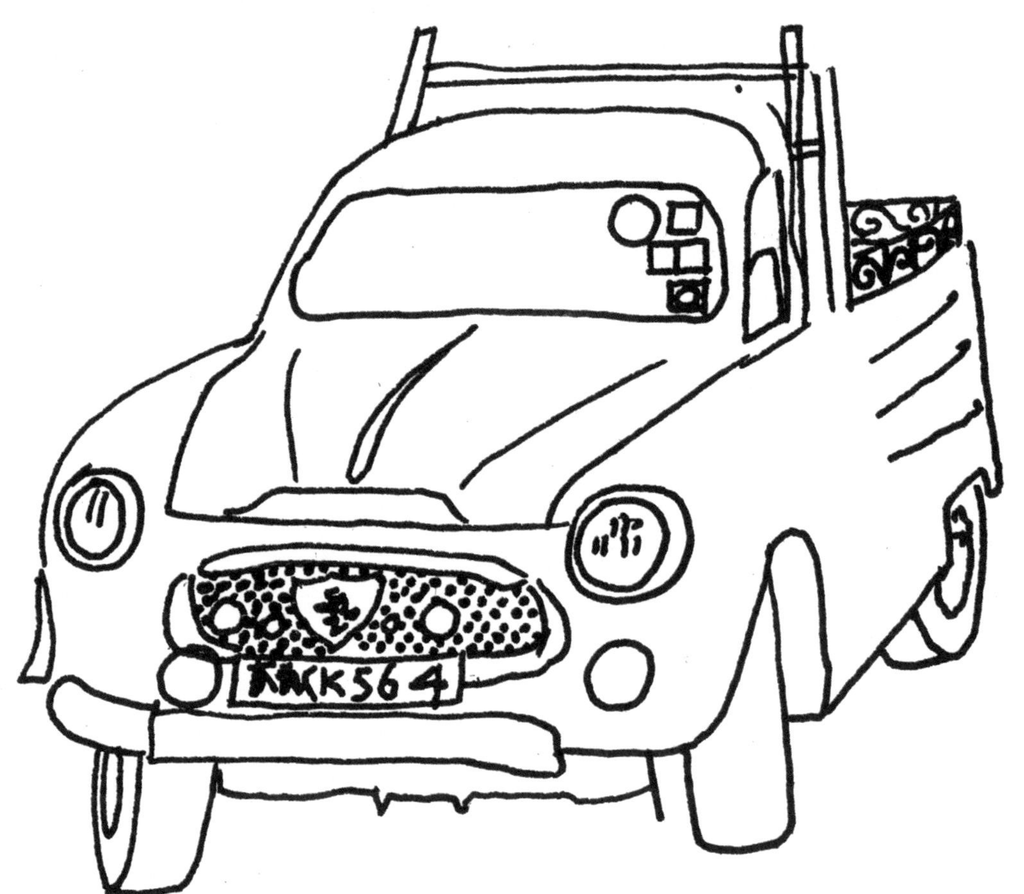

NEW MASTER JERRY

HAIRCUTS SALON

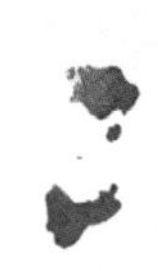

MUSHY E. MUSHY

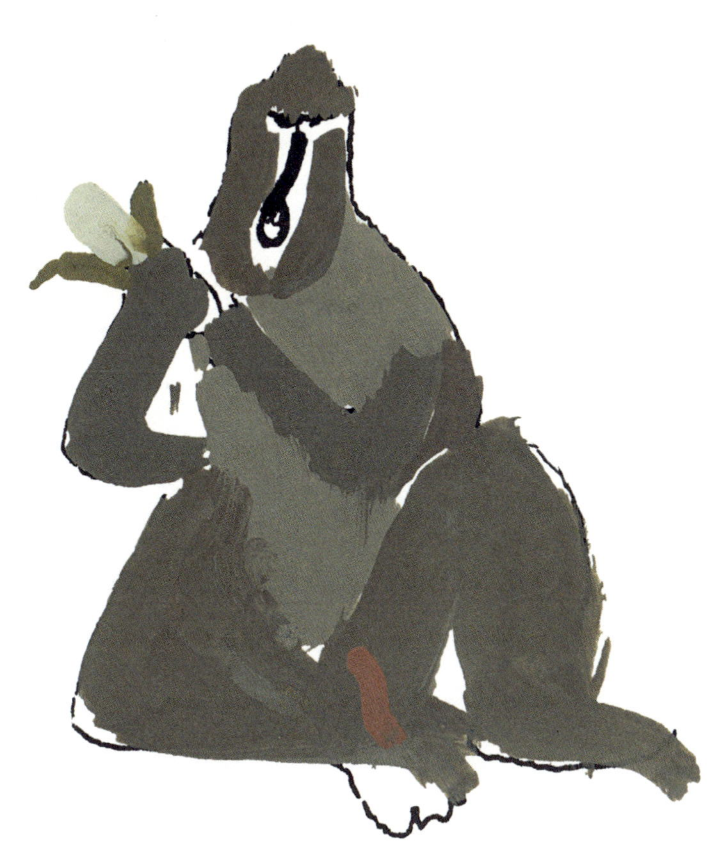

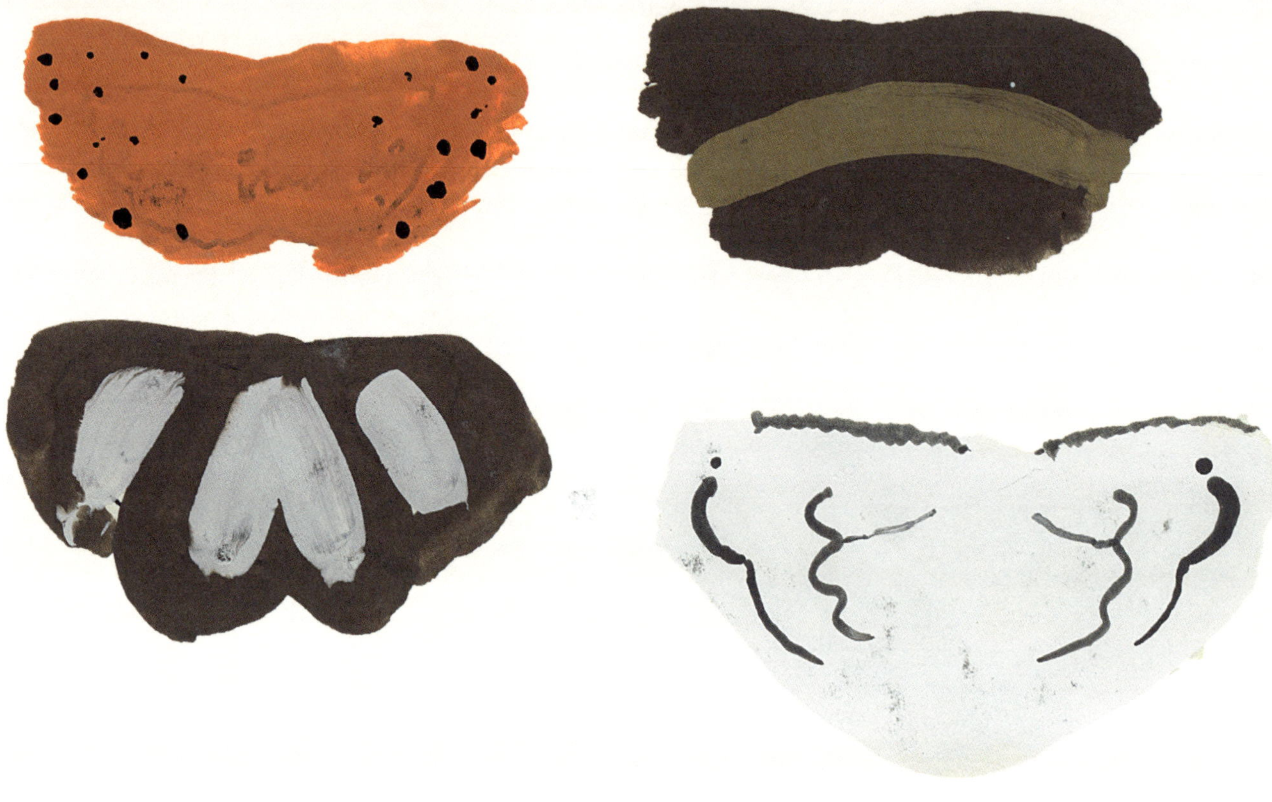

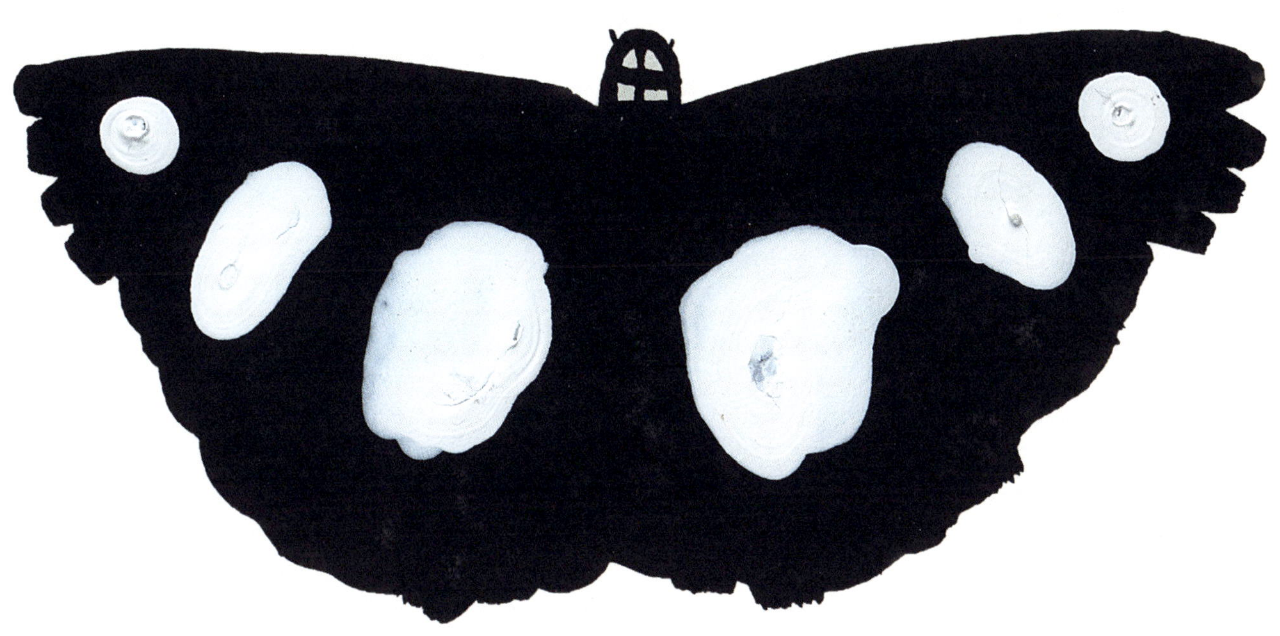

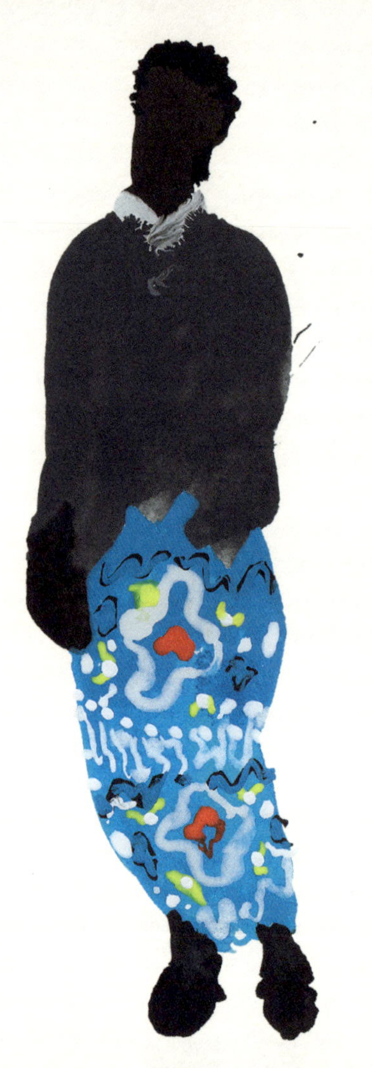

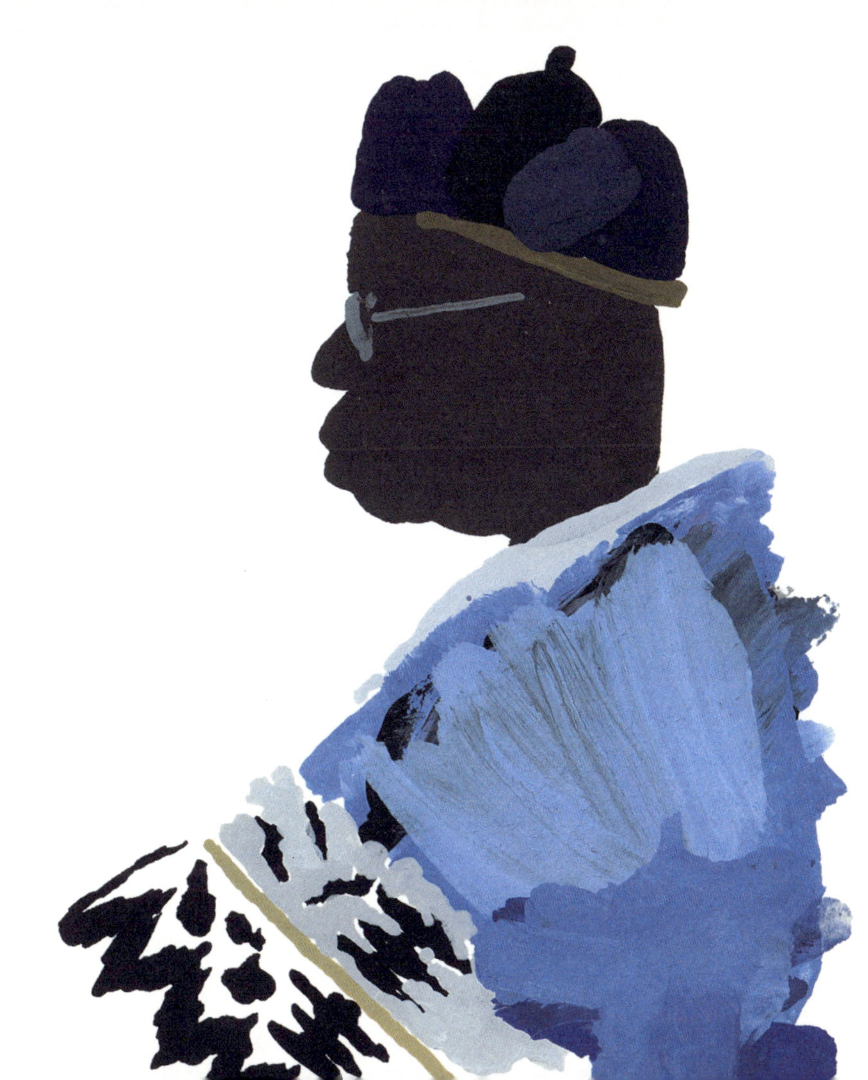

Sun 2 March
up at the crack, light breakfast then to a Kikuyu mass in the local church (catholic) which had a political play staged by a young man in a suit tie & porkpie hat, a man in a hat raincoat shiny black gumboots and a gnarled walking stick & 4 others. Shiny boots made a good entrance but thereafter failed to deliver. Pork pie made all the running. It is all ad lib but not carefully enough rehearsed. Apparently on a good Sunday the whole church is in uproar. Good place to take note of the clothing. Some very good jumpers. All secondhand gear but beautiful colours plum reds lemon yellow grey brown & purple. Afterwards many people come up to Rachel. I am introduced as the brother, same mother same father. Only one asks if I am, well, who is the oldest. We are invited for tea at Joseph and Margaret's who drive a rough old Peugeot but are wealthy Kikuyus.

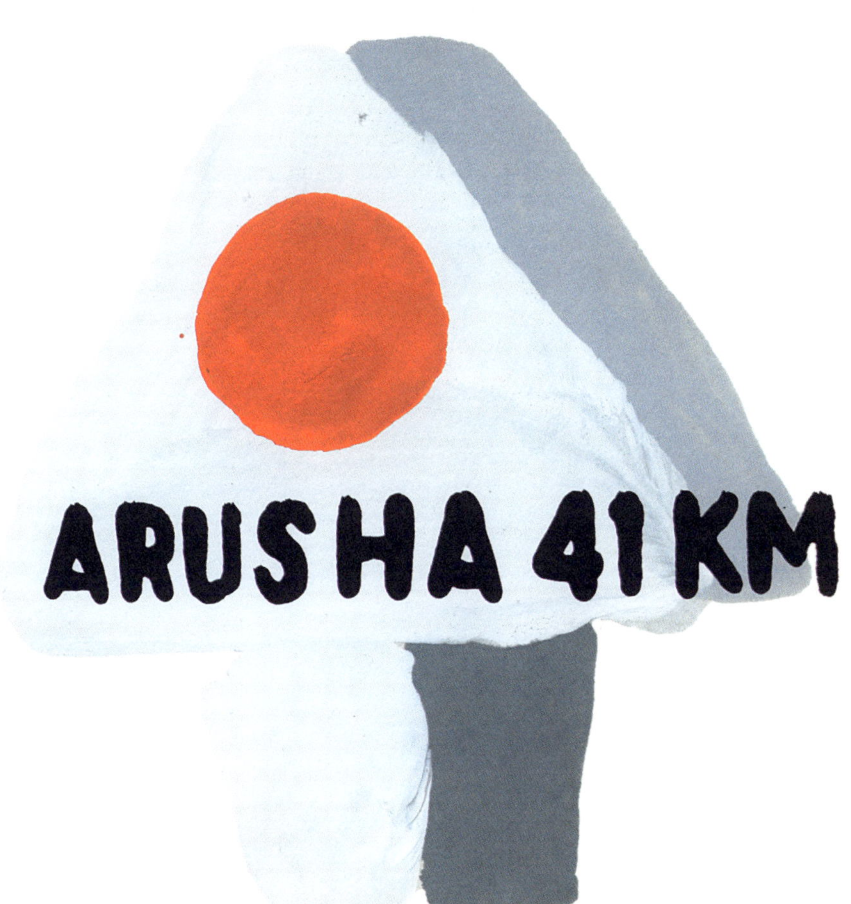
ARUSHA 41 KM

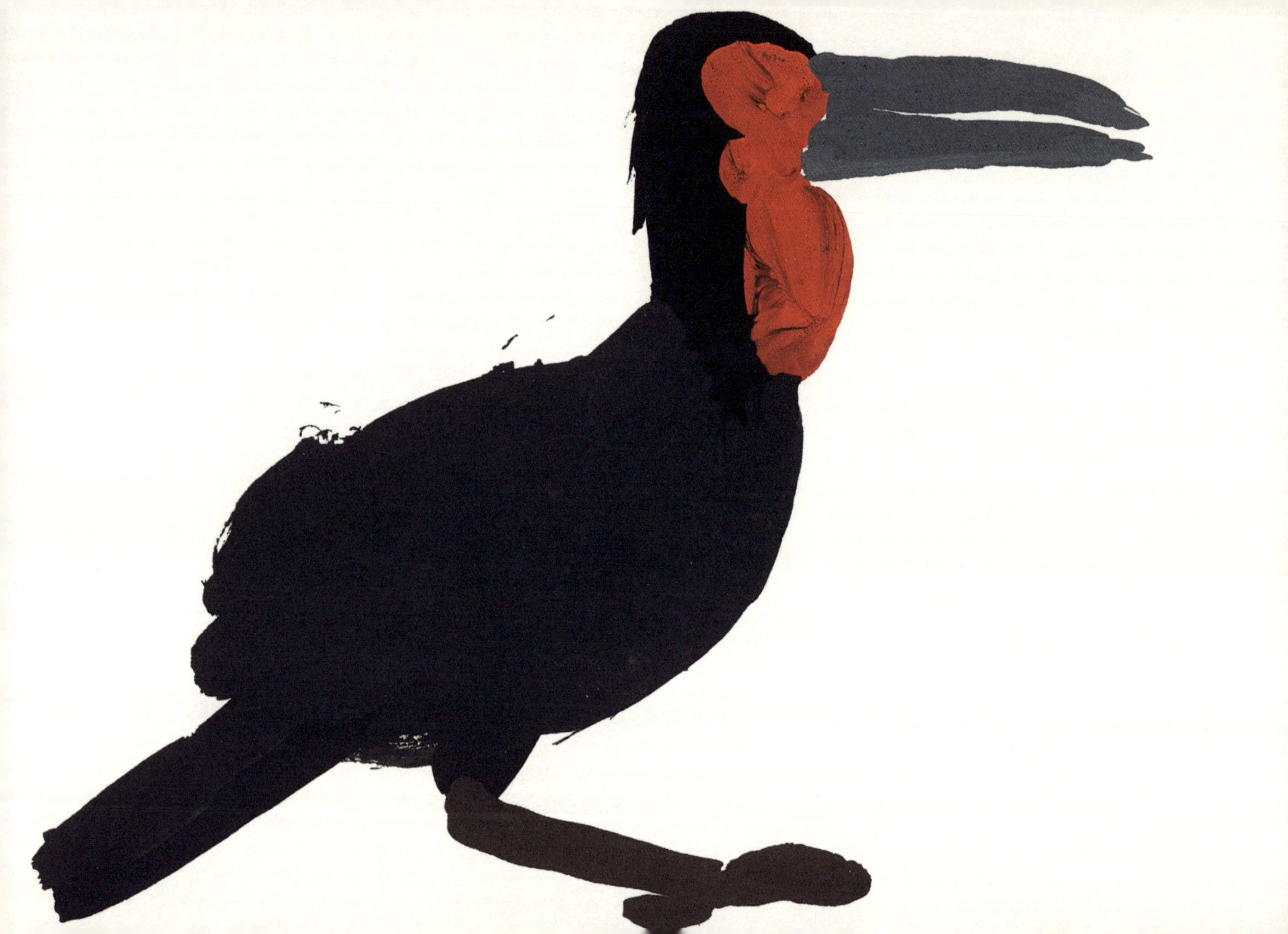

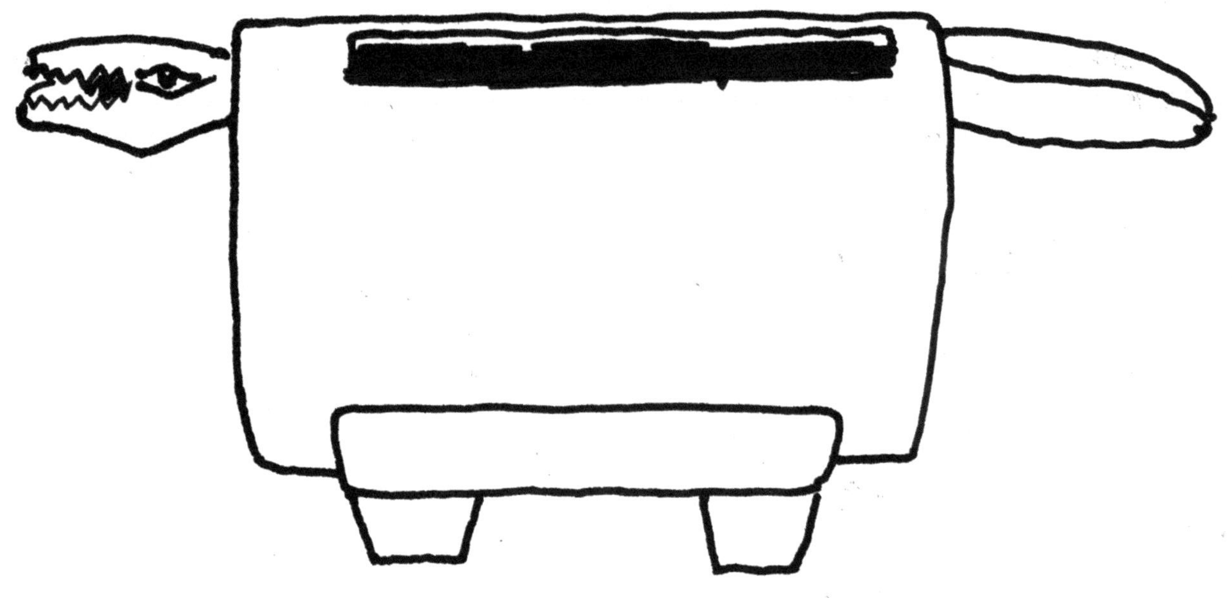

TELEPHONE

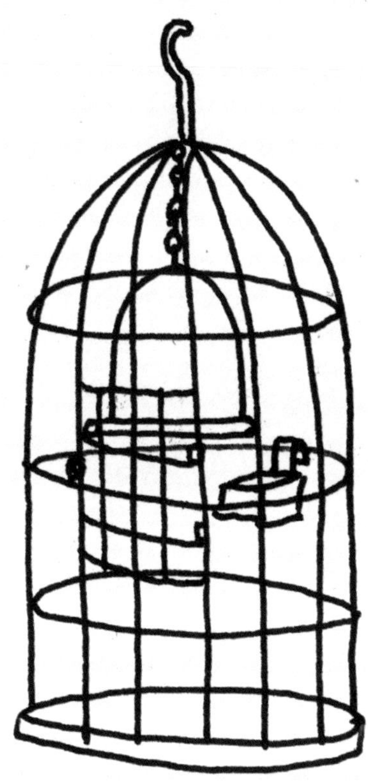

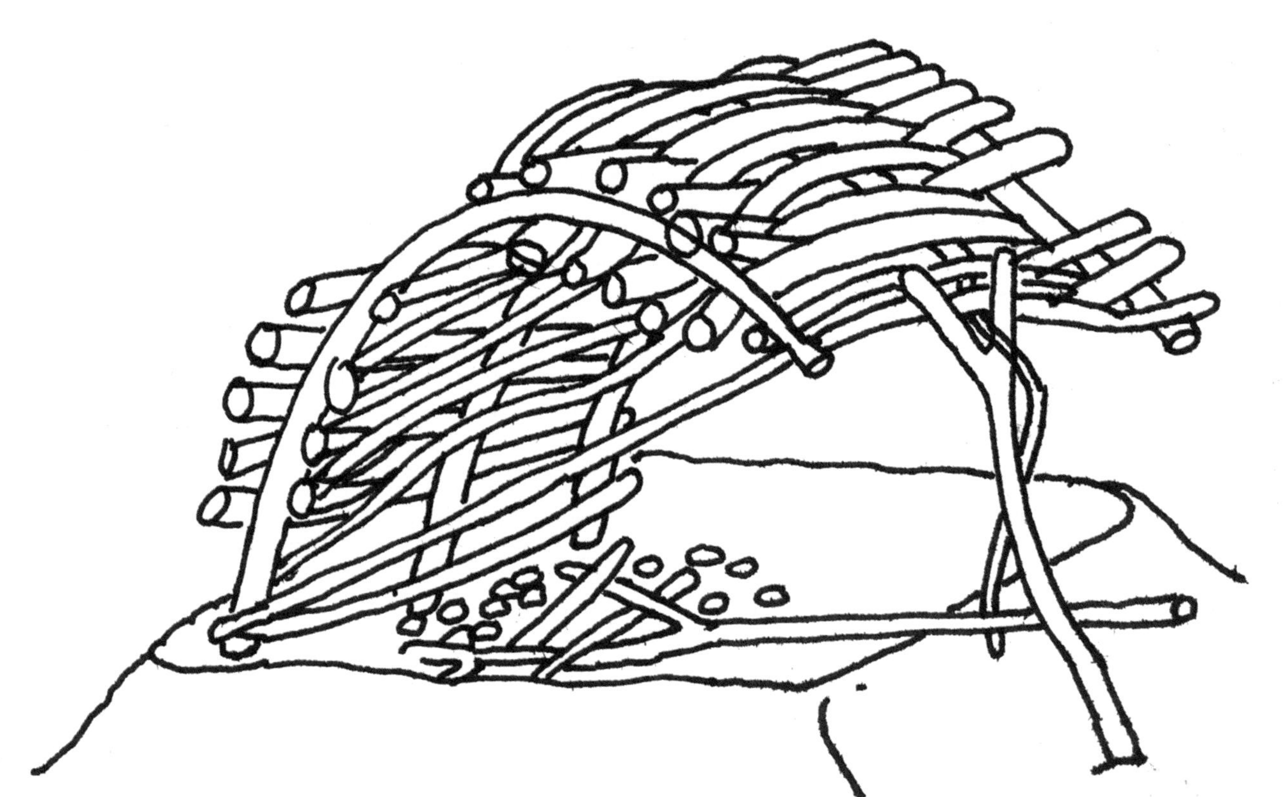

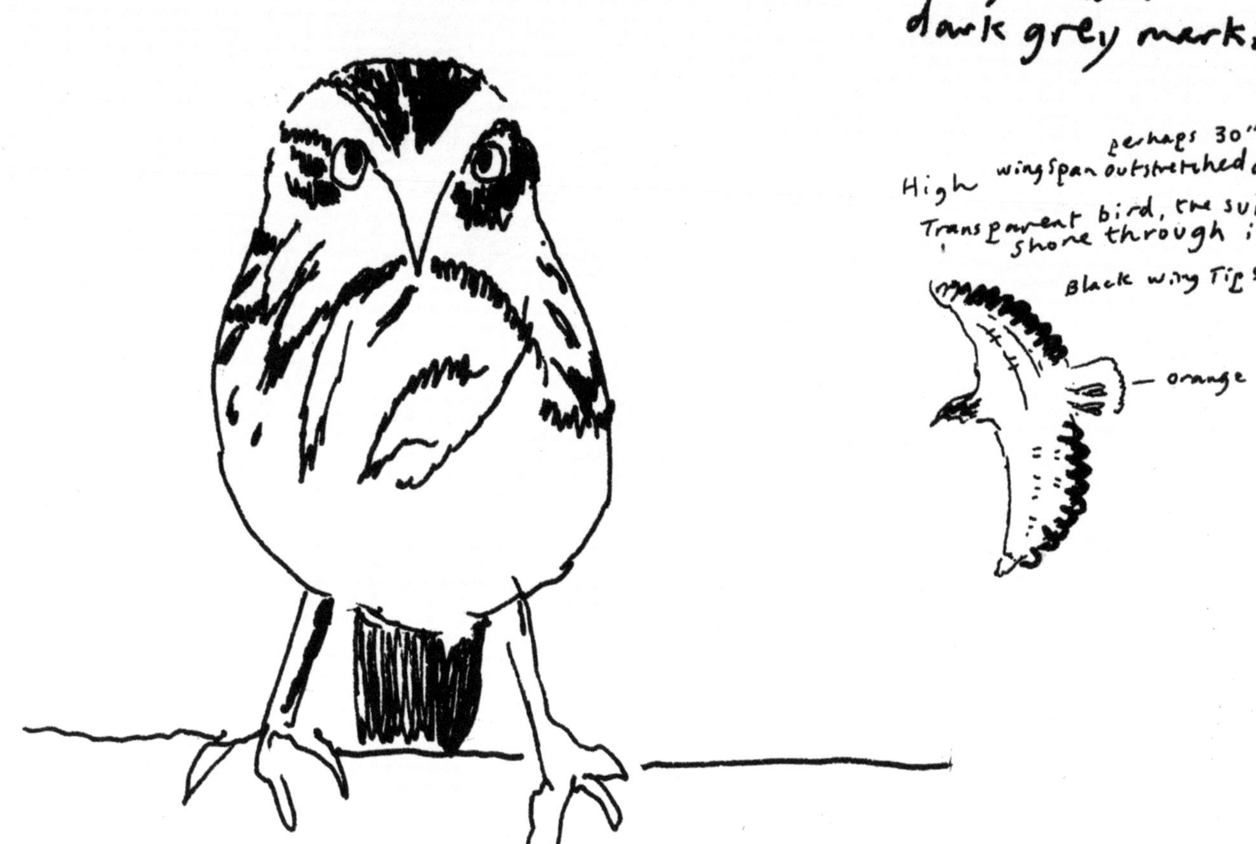

STREAKY SEEDEATER

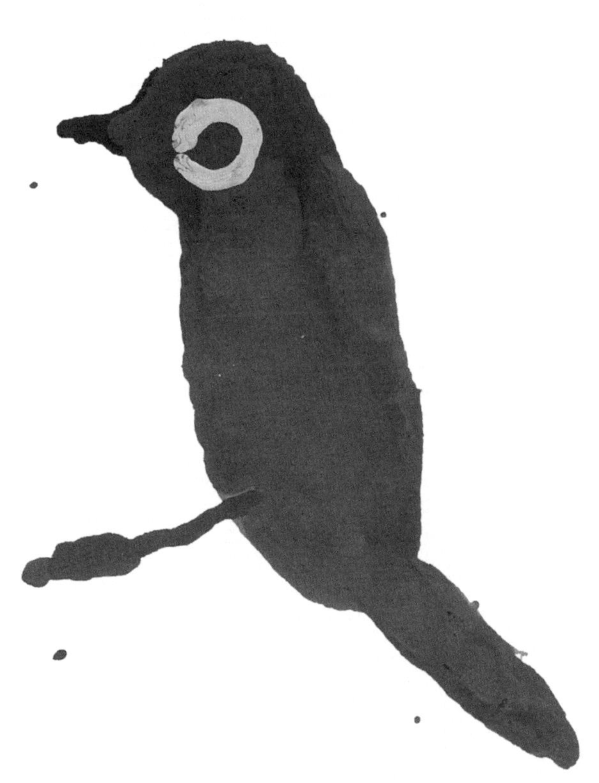

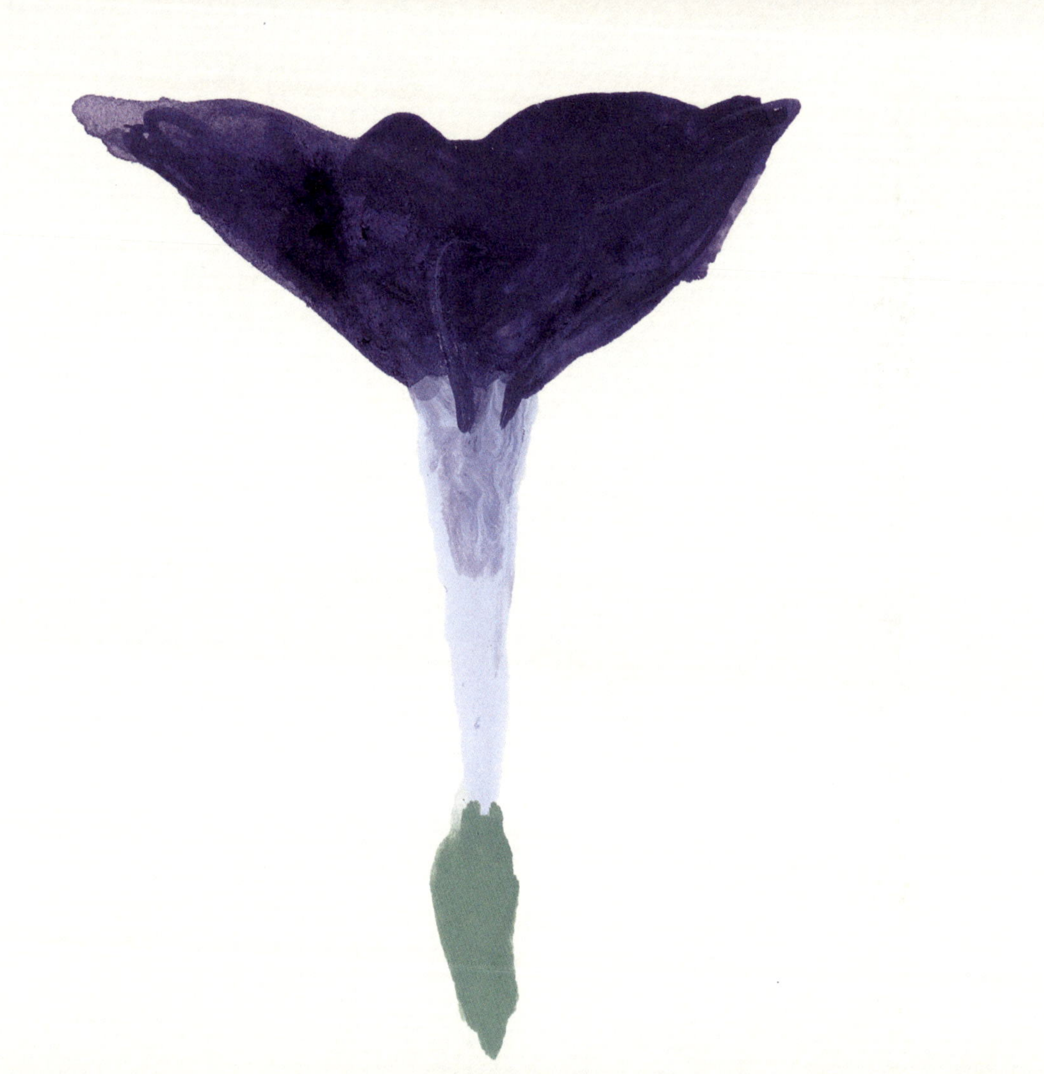

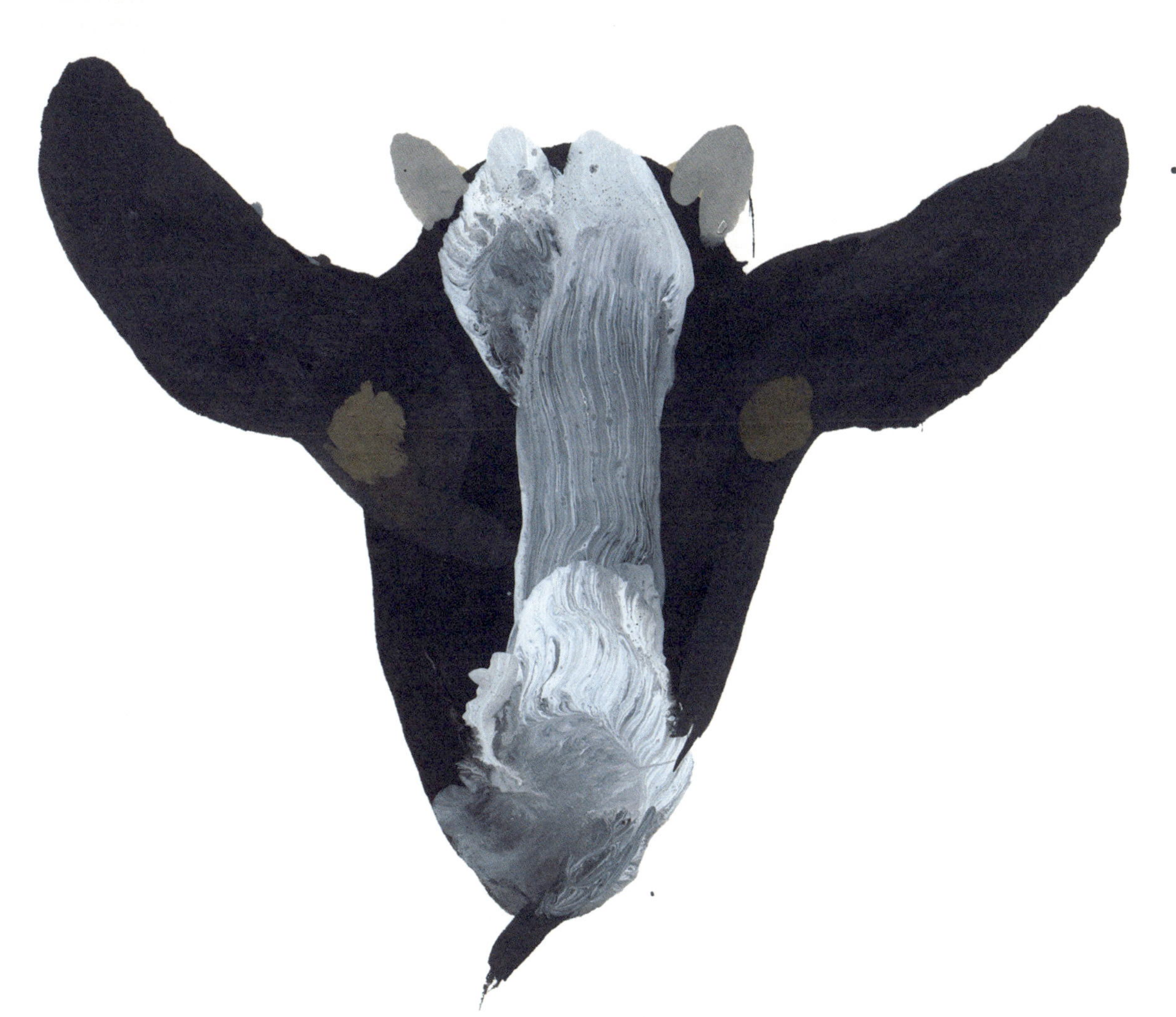

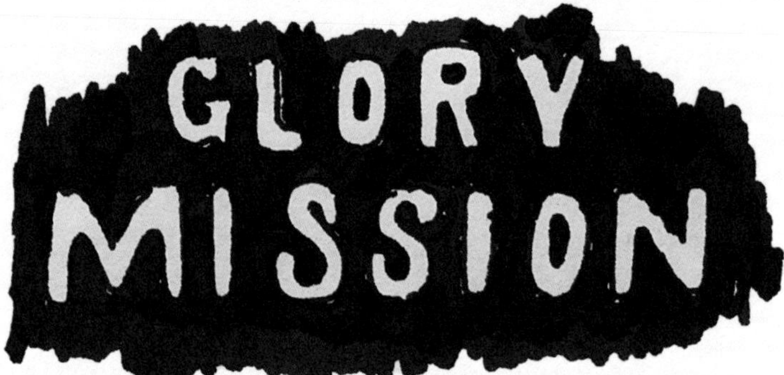
GLORY
MISSION

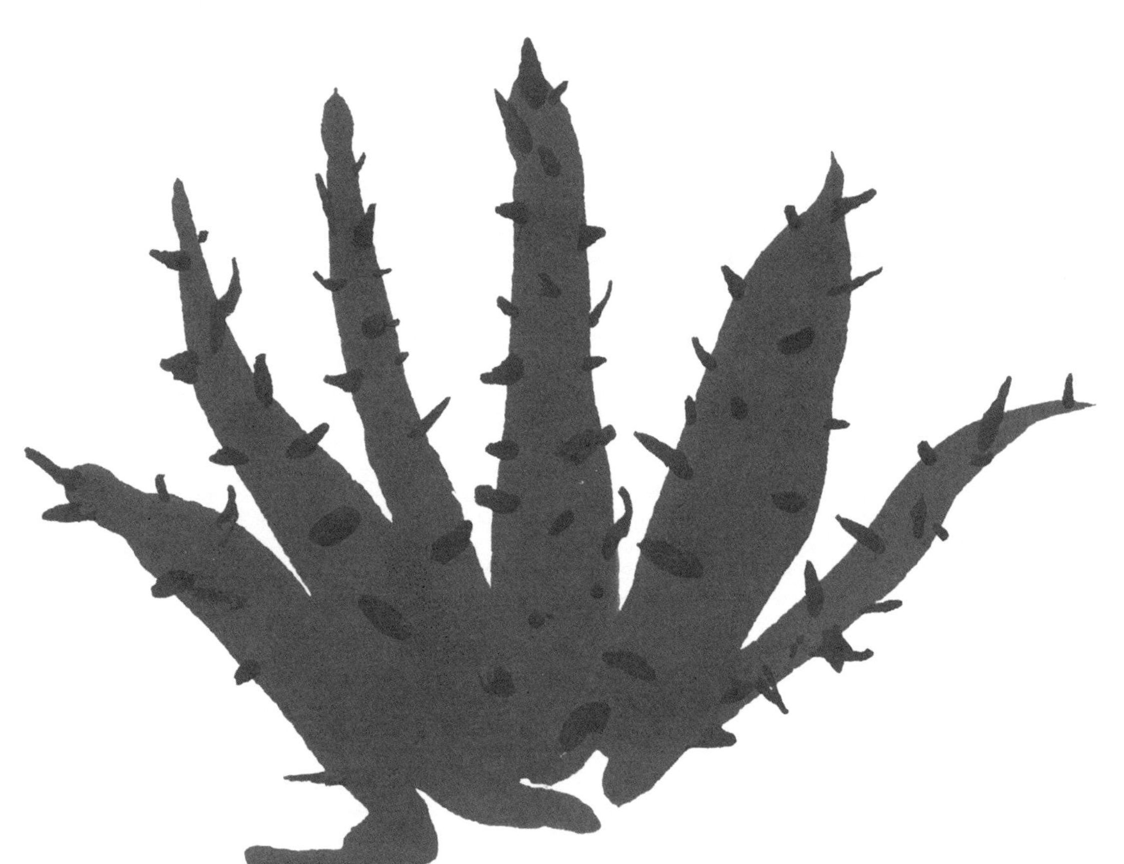

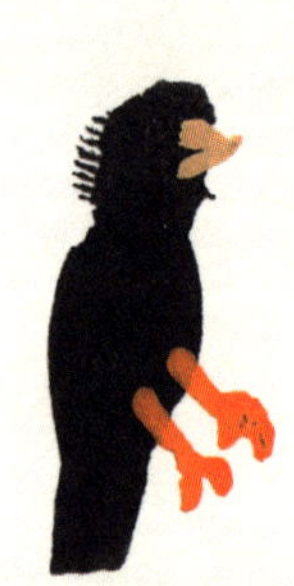

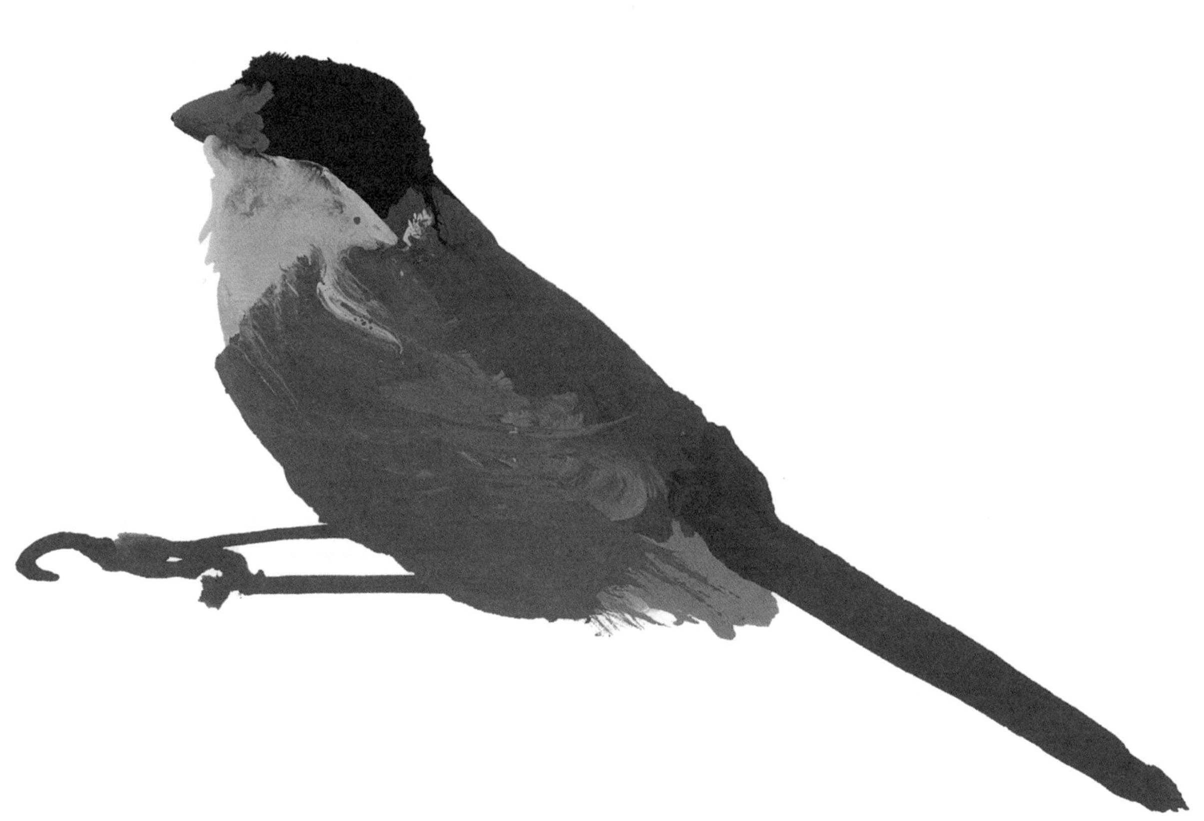

PRIVATE
RESIDENCE

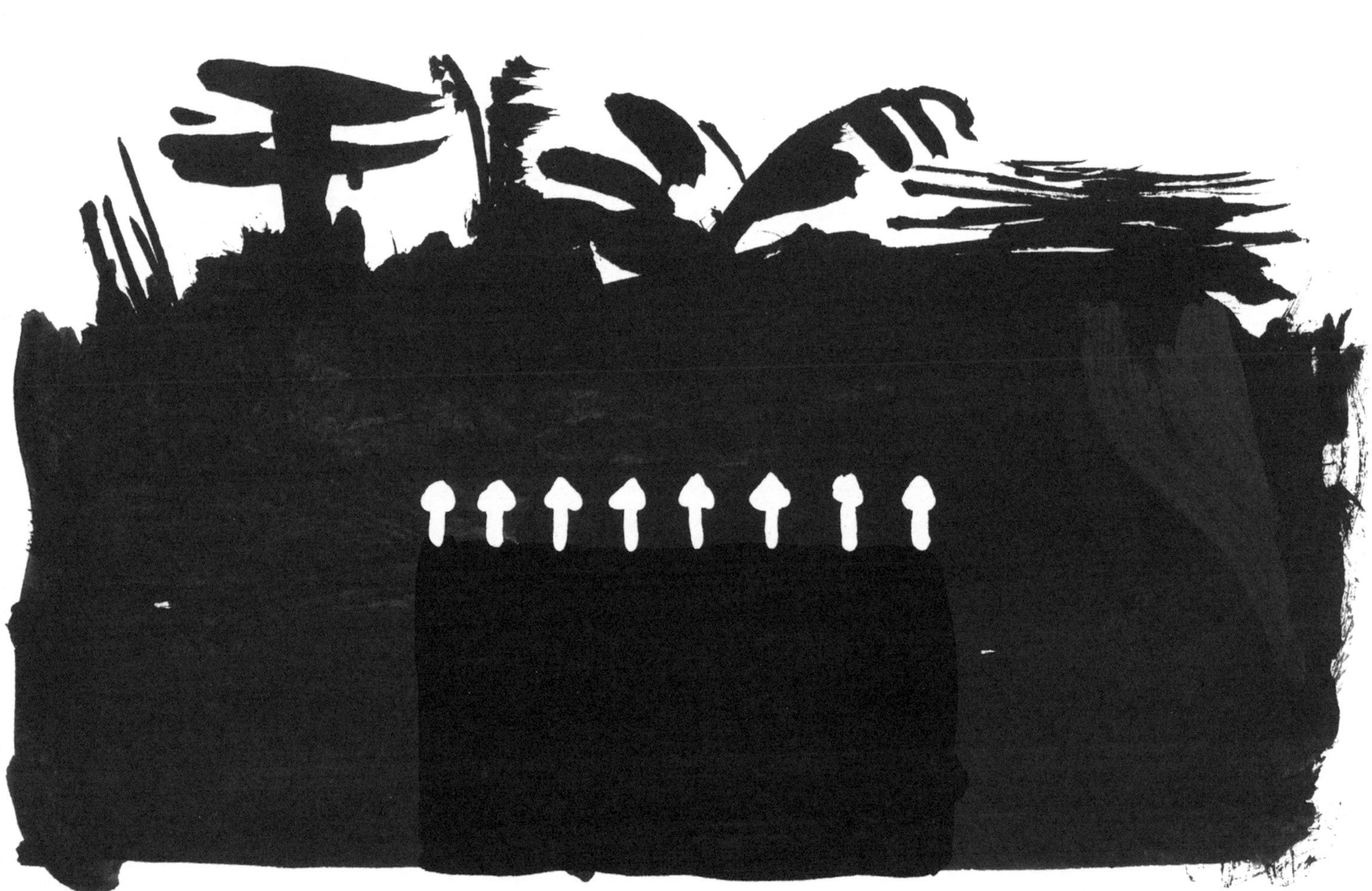

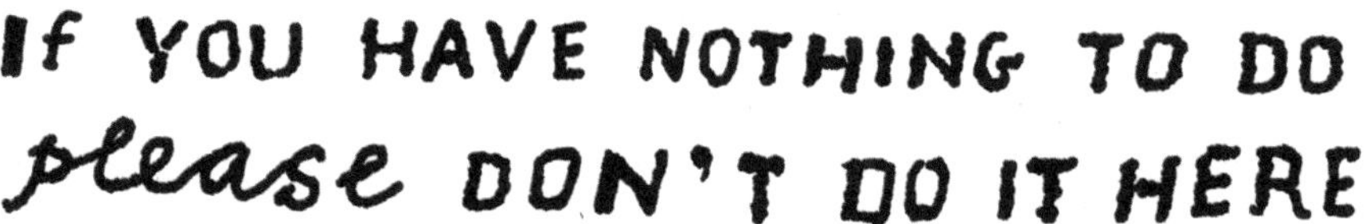
IF YOU HAVE NOTHING TO DO
please DON'T DO IT HERE

ROYAL ACADEMY PUBLICATIONS
Florence Dassonville, Production and Distribution Co-ordinator
Carola Krueger, Production and Distribution Manager
Peter Sawbridge, Head of Publishing and Editorial Director

Studio Co-ordination: Beatrice Butler-Bowdon
Photography: Mike Bruce
Design: Maggi Smith
Printed in Wales by Gomer Press

Royal Academy of Arts
Burlington House
Piccadilly
London W1J 0BD
www.royalacademy.org.uk

EU Authorised Representative
EAS Europe, Mustamäe tee 50, 10621 Tallinn, Estonia
gpsr.requests@easproject.com

British Library Cataloguing-in-Publication Data
A catalogue record for this book is available from the British Library

ISBN 978-1-915815-14-9

Distributed outside the United States and Canada by
ACC Art Books Ltd, Riverside House, Dock Lane, Melton,
Woodbridge, IP12 1PE

Distributed in the United States and Canada by
ARTBOOK | D.A.P., 75 Broad Street, Suite 630, New York, NY 10004

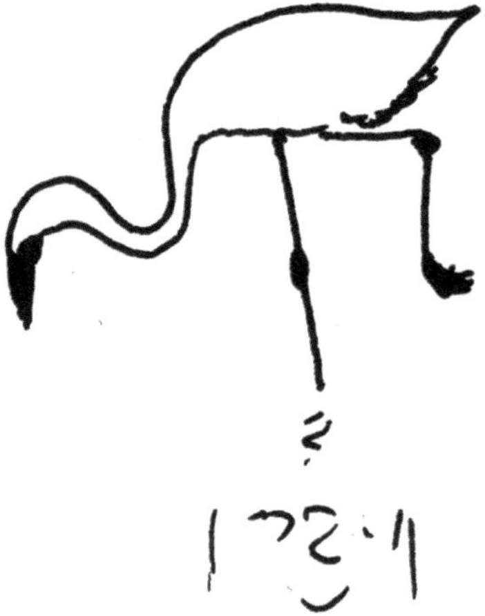

ACKNOWLEDGEMENTS

This book is for Rachel.

At the Royal Academy, Peter Sawbridge originally broached the idea, my books into a book, and oversaw. Carola Krueger and Florence Dassonville watchfully and patiently made it happen. The designer Maggi Smith conjured how it looks. With what I can only describe as singular understanding, Mike Bruce has photographed my work for thirty years. I could not have done any of it without the eye and hand of my daughter Beatrice. Once again, the lucid presence of Randy Lerner hovers. His generosity made it possible. I thank them all.

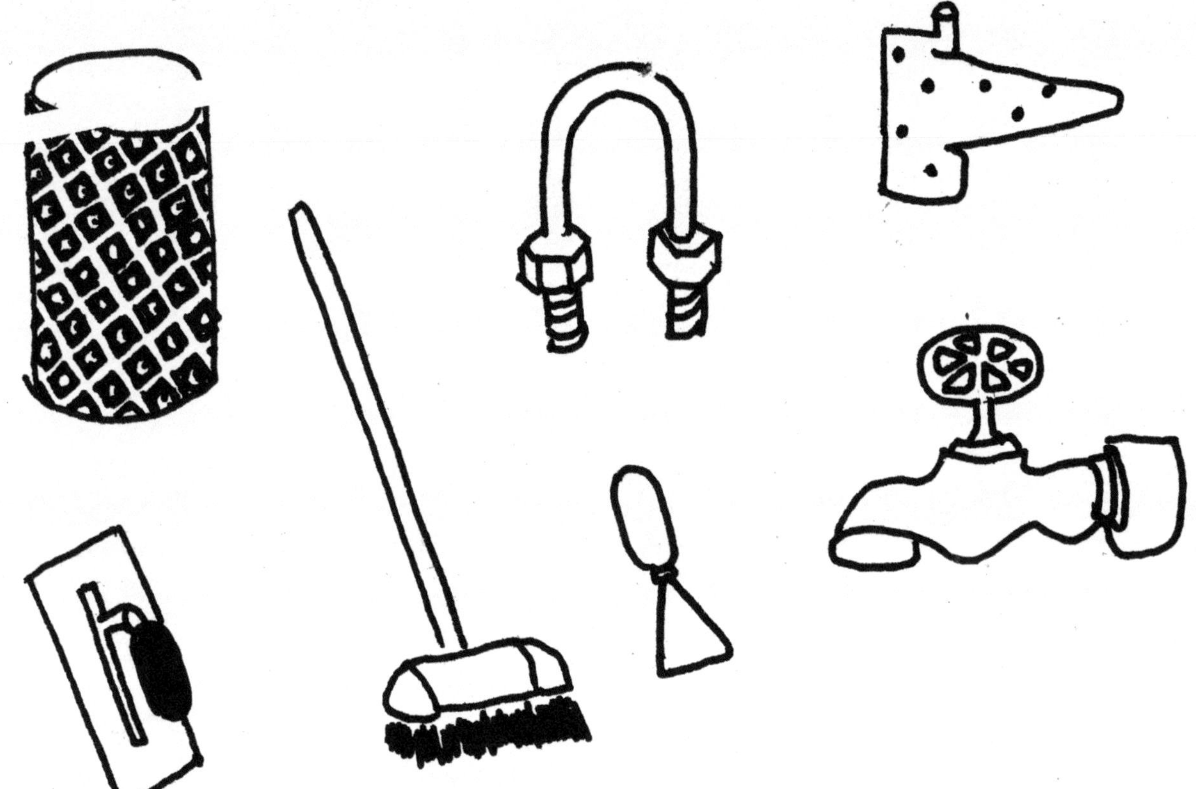